RENEWALS 691-4574

DATE DUE

APR 20

Demco, Inc. 38-293

THINKING NEW ABOUT
SOVIET "NEW THINKING"

RESEARCH SERIES/NUMBER 74

Thinking New About Soviet "New Thinking"

V. Kubálková &
A. A. Cruickshank

INSTITUTE
OF INTERNATIONAL
STUDIES
University of California, Berkeley

Library of Congress Cataloging-in-Publication Data

Kubálková, V.
  Thinking new about Soviet "new thinking" /
V. Kubálková & A. A. Cruickshank.
     p. cm. — (Research series, ISSN 0068-6093 ; no. 74)
  Includes bibliographical references.
    1. Soviet Union—Foreign relations—1985– .
2. Perestroika. 3. Soviet Union—Study and
teaching—United States. I. Cruickshank, A. A. II. Title.
III. Series: Research series (University of California,
Berkeley, Institute of International Studies) ; no. 74.
DK289.K82 1989   327.47—dc20   89-20002
ISBN 0-87725-174-6

Printed in the United States of America

CONTENTS

ACKNOWLEDGMENTS

The work on this project predates the Gorbachev era. The Australian government (ARGS) funded Kubálková's research dealing with Soviet attempts to change international law as a method of changing the international order, and as it transpired, the Soviet notion of "New International Law" anticipated the much more broadly conceived "New Thinking." It is therefore thanks to the ARGS that the authors were able to recognize the meaning of "New Thinking" almost immediately upon the arrival of the concept in the West. With the passage of time, the main thesis of this study has become less controversial, but when Kubálková first came to the United States as an Australian Senior Fulbright Scholar in 1987–88 and presented her interpretation of "New Thinking," many Sovietologists expressed shock. The benefit derived by the authors from subsequent critical discussions at Stanford, Berkeley, USC, UCLA, and the Rand Corporation was invaluable.

Our thanks go particularly to the Hoover Institution, Stanford University, the University of California at Berkeley, and the University of Miami. The study developed from a series of public lectures sponsored by the Center for Russian and East European Studies at Stanford in January 1988 when Kubálková, as a Senior Research Fellow at Stanford and Visiting Scholar at Hoover, collected much of the material. The early version took shape with the assistance of the Institute of International Studies at Berkeley, where Kubálková was a Research Scholar, and the final version was written during a Visiting Professorship at the Graduate School of International Studies (Institute of Soviet and East European Studies), University of Miami.

Of the individuals whose comments on various drafts and/or encouragement were particularly helpful, we would like to acknowledge Professor Carl Rosberg, Director of the Institute of International Studies at Berkeley, his Principal Editor, Paul Gilchrist, and the anonymous readers of the manuscript. Our thanks are due also to

Professors Kenneth N. Waltz, James N. Rosenau, Robert O. Keohane, Andrzej Korbonski, Alexander Dallin, Jan F. Triska, Ambler Moss Jr., Enrique Baloyra, A. H. McIntire, and Jiri Valenta. This is of course in no way to shirk responsibility for any mistakes or the main theses of this study, which we share only with the Soviet "new thinkers."

We dedicate this study to the faculty and students of the Graduate School of International Studies at the University of Miami in recognition of their unfailing encouragement and receptivity to the idea of the West "thinking new" about Soviet "New Thinking."

V. K.
A. A. C.

Summer 1989
Coral Gables, Florida

Chapter 1

INTRODUCTION:
"NEW THINKING" ON INTERNATIONAL
RELATIONS *QUA* THINKING

Few events in this century have stirred the world's imagination as much as the changes afoot in the USSR since Mikhail Gorbachev's ascent to power in 1985. The Russian words *perestroika* ("restructuring") and *glasnost* ("openness") have become a part of most languages across the globe. They carry implications for the rest of us, with much hope and expectation attached to their meaning.

The third of Gorbachev's three main catchwords—*novoe myshlenie* ("new thinking") on international relations—has as a concept received less attention in the West.* This attitude is consistent with Western skepticism in the past toward Soviet thinking and writing. The bewilderment engendered by the appearance of "new thinking" is reflected in the variety of responses to it, ranging from those who

---

NOTE: Soviet and Western sources relating directly to "New Thinking" are listed in Appendixes 1 and 2; references to them throughout the text are in author-date citation style. All other sources are cited in full in footnotes.

*As Robert Legvold, chairman of the Task Force on Soviet New Thinking and director of the Harriman Institute for Advanced Study of the Soviet Union at Columbia University, puts it: "It is important when considering the foreign policy implications of Gorbachev's initiatives and statements *not to focus unduly on the concept of "new thinking" as such*, which has been advanced by Gorbachev and his associates as a general rubric for the General Secretary's approach to international affairs. Any new thinking takes place within a historical context of adaptation by the Soviet leadership to external realities. It is this broader pattern, and not any particular slogan, that should be the focus of Western attention. . . . The "new thinking" label itself confounds understanding more than it helps, and it might be better to set it aside and look for formulations that have more solidity and focus" (Legvold 1988: 4, 8; emphasis added). The task force's report, *How Should America Respond to Gorbachev's Challenge?*, was published in 1987 by the Institute for East-West Security studies, jointly with the Foreign Policy Association, and subsequently as a small book (Legvold 1988).

1

claim it is old Communist ideology in newly labelled bottles to those who rejoice in the "de-ideologization" of the USSR. The Western scales have tipped in favor of the latter view, and any effort to investigate seriously the possibility of a position between these two extremes—and study "new thinking" *qua* thinking—seems to be inhibited by a continuing fear of cold war associations.

The reason most frequently adduced for the prevailing approach, which often prevents discussion of "new thinking," derives from the view that the primary impetus for Gorbachev's reform program is domestic and not international. Hence the subordinate conceptual role of thinking about international relations—an "afterthought" in Gorbachev's calculations. Certainly the statistics of Soviet economic performance and documents issuing from important CPSU meetings since the 1985 April plenary session of the party Central Committee* would seem to confirm that the main objective was not to "restructure" international relations, but rather the restructuring of society in a superpower that by 1985 found itself in serious socioeconomic crisis. "New thinking" has, then been conceived of as an adjunct of perestroika and perhaps as one of the means of its achievement.†

At a minimum its task has been seen as the encouragement of a stable, tranquil international environment conducive to the implementation of drastic domestic change—at an optimum, as enlisting Western support for advancing the process. It is not difficult to appreciate what benefits for perestroika would flow from the input of Western technology and massive infusions of capital, to say nothing of the advantages of escaping (or more correctly, helping to defray) the crippling costs of engagement in an advanced weapons systems race.

Thus with Gorbachev widely assumed to have de-ideologized his foreign policy,** Soviet "new thinking" on international relations

*Soviet writers attribute the setting in motion of the reform movement to this occasion.

†"The 27th CPSU Congress and the subsequent plenary sessions of the Central Committee have defined *the main instruments* of accelerating development as the democratization of all spheres of the vital activity of Soviet society. Openness, criticism, self-criticism, emancipation, the abandonment of the presumption of infallibility—all this, initially directed inward, has also been reflected in the practice of working out and implementing our state's foreign-policy course" (Primakov 1987: 2; emphasis added).

**For example, Sestanovich thinks that Gorbachev has freed "Soviet foreign policy from ideological preoccupations and constraints" (1988: 5).

is treated by some commentators simply as something "a bit like propaganda," and it occupies a subordinate place in the minds of those in the West who have sought to interpret each new stage in the process of Soviet change. Although "new" Soviet foreign policy obviously has more *direct* importance for the outside world than the eventual improvement of living conditions inside the Soviet Union, it is assumed in the West that Soviet foreign policy will improve virtually automatically with internal change in the USSR in a positive direction.

Gorbachev himself encouraged this attitude when he subordinated Soviet foreign policy to domestic reform. On one occasion he claimed to have forgotten who before him had made the connection between domestic and foreign policy;* Marx and Lenin were among those who had.† In the West there is continuing argument about whether or not to help Gorbachev by accepting his foreign policy initiatives and/or by massive transfusions of economic (especially technological) assistance.**

"New thinking" has shown itself to have a life of its own, however, and the hope it inspires and its vague implications of goodwill precede its elucidation. In contrast to domestic perestroika,

---

*On the eve of the Geneva summit, Gorbachev remarked in an interview: "I don't remember who, but somebody said that foreign policy is a continuation of domestic policy. If that is so, then I ask you to ponder one thing: if we in the Soviet Union are setting ourselves such truly grandiose plans in the domestic sphere, then what are the external conditions that we need to be able to fulfill these domestic plans? I leave the answer to that question with you" (*Time*, 9 September 1985). In a similar vein he declared at the world peace forum in Moscow: "Our international policy is, more than ever, determined by our internal policy, by our interest in concentrating on creative work to make our country more perfect. Precisely for this reason we need stable peace, predictability, and a constructive orientation in international relations" (*Pravda*, 17 February 1987; cited in Dallin 1987: 23).

†This connection is encapsulated for Western students of international relations in the "second image" of Kenneth Waltz. In his influential study *Man, the State and War* (New York, 1959), Waltz classifies the writings of political philosophers on the causes of war into those who see it as originating in the nature of man (first image), those who believe it to result from the ways in which states are constituted (second image), and those who find its origins in the nature of the society of states (third image).

**For further discussion of the linkage between domestic and foreign policy, see ch. 5 below (pp. 100–3).

which has shown little or no success thus far, Soviet "new" foreign policy has been the only area of Soviet reform to show significant results. Several of the principles associated with "new thinking" are finding their way into international treaties and other documents and have been adopted by the UN General Assembly. Third World leaders, Western political figures, and a train of foreign scholars on visits to a suddenly hospitable USSR generously compliment the Soviets on their "new thinking" and enthusiastically endorse whatever they understand it to be.

The Soviets' own usages have not assisted in clarifying this controversial and elusive concept. After an apparently late start in the Soviet Union, the term *novoe myshlenie* experienced a rapid surge in popularity that has marked its progress since, and yet as late as August 1986 the Soviet deputy foreign minister appeared not to quite know what it means.* In the USSR, as in the West, as a result of its use interchangeably with other key words and catch phrases, "new thinking" has undergone a confusing extension of meaning. Gorbachev himself makes references to perestroika *of international relations*, and in much the same way "new thinking" has become simply synonymous with his reform package to include domestic perestroika, glasnost, and anything else that is "new," no matter how remote from international relations.† The injunction to "think new" has become a new imperative that refers not only to international politics but punctuates Soviet political discourse, and Soviet leaders would clearly like it to stand as the *Zeitgeist* of their era. "New thinking" now applies to both domestic reform and international relations, with the former, broader application hampering close investigation of the latter.

We deal here with "new thinking" as a concept of international relations, in which sense attempts at understanding have so far been sadly lacking or too soon abandoned. In explanation of this failure, Dallin observes that "despite repeated endorsement . . . we would

---

*Interviewed on Hungarian television, Vladimir Petrovskij confirmed that there was "a new type of thinking," but when pressed as to what this meant he made only general references to "promoting cooperation and mutual understanding" and to Moscow's "realistic proposals" ("Moscow's Foreign Policy Initiatives," *Soviet Analyst* 15, no. 16 [13 August 1986]).

†For example, Burlatsky's book entitled *Novoe myshlenie* (1988) has a great deal more to say on Soviet domestic policy than on international relations.

look in vain for a formal Soviet summation of its defining features" and as a concept "new thinking" is "inchoate and untidy" (1987: 22, 6). A similar vagueness is encountered in the half-hearted attempts to define and understand the "old thinking" that the "new thinking" purportedly supplants. Snyder (1987/88) takes "old thinking" to mean the "atavisms" of Brezhnev and others, while Legvold sees "new thinking" as "a change of mind" and "maybe a cynical, empty slogan," since "people, let alone whole governments, do not suddenly begin thinking differently because someone announces they should" (1988: 8). The point to be made here is that, generally speaking, Western definitions of the meaning of "new thinking" (see Appendix 2) vary substantially.*

Associations of the Term "New Thinking" in Soviet Texts

In circumstances of mystery surrounding its meaning, we shall attempt to examine the Soviets' own understanding of the concept of "new thinking." We shall start with analysis of their usage of the term and its associations. A scrutiny of Soviet texts makes it clear that the term is not used exclusively to refer to departures from pre-Gorbachev, pre-reform thinking;[†] it refers to the "thinking of humanity in the nuclear age," in the sense first used by Albert Einstein—a point that has either escaped Western analysts or is not regarded as important enough to deserve comment. We find that Soviet sources that refer to "new thinking" or "new political thinking" on international relations invariably single out for mention one or more of some ten associated concepts. Only a few Soviet sources[**] (and even fewer Western commentaries[††]) refer to all ten, but Soviet

*Berner and Dahm 1987/1988; Dallin 1987; Evangelista 1987; Glickham 1986; Legvold 1988a, 1988b; Light 1987a, 1987b, 1988; Meissner 1986; Miller 1988; Sestanovich 1988; Shenfield 1987; Snyder 1987/88; Valkenier 1987; Wettig 1987; Zhi and Zhang 1988.

[†]When the excesses of previous Soviet foreign policy are criticized, for example, by Gorbachev in his political report to the 27th CPSU Congress (Gorbachev 1987a), the "old thinking" that is rejected is mainly not Soviet but Western thinking.

[**]For example, Shevardnadze 1988b; Gorbachev 1988f.

[††]Margot Light (1988) identifies six, Dallin (1987) four, Glickham (1986) about seven, Snyder (1987/88) none, and Legvold (1988) about three, suggesting

sources always cite some or all of the following principles (in various combinations (and in no particular order):

1. Identification with the global problems of mankind, or "global human problems" (nuclear catastrophe, ecological disaster, poverty, etc.);
2. Concept of the interdependence for survival of mankind in a world regarded as one interrelated totality;
3. Renunciation of war (there is therefore no substance to "Soviet threat"!), with
4. Concept of peace as the highest of humanity's values;
5. Security of all states regarded as global, indivisible, and
6. Attainable not by military but by political means on the basis not of "balance of power" but of "balance of interests" in a comprehensive system of security;
7. Reduction in the level of military confrontation in all areas;
8. Size of military arsenals to be based on "reasonable sufficiency" to repel aggression, with
9. Stress on flexibility in international relations so as to reflect their realistic assessment;
10. One interrelated and interdependent world of coexisting socialism and capitalism. (The mode of thought continuing to distinguish socialism from capitalism is Marxist-Leninist historical materialism based on dialectics.)

Interpretations

The fact that "new thinking" is associated with a number of the principles summarized above presents a problem. These points

---

instead his own idiosyncratic, four-point interpretation of the meaning of Soviet "new thinking" that is based on analysis of changed Soviet attitudes in regard to (1) security, (2) interdependence, (3) the Third World, and (4) socialist states. According to Sestanovich, "new thinking" includes "a devaluation of ideological precepts, a more complacent assessment of outside threats, a re-examination of national interests and a heavier stress on global 'common' interests, a cap on resource commitments, a search for less expensive policy instruments, a more flexible and less demanding stance in negotiations, and arms-length attitude toward friends in need and an insistence that they do more to help themselves, avoidance of actions that adversaries can treat as provocations, and so forth" (1988: 4).

are clearly of differing degrees of generality; as a result, the method adopted by Western writers in analyzing them has been piecemeal, with perhaps a special focus on new foreign policy (with point 9 as the basic premise), or on a new Soviet doctrine of national security (points 5–9), or on other areas, such as arms control, as these commend themselves to the interest of the individual commentator. Where a number of points are mentioned, their ordering affects the understanding of their logic: points 1–4 placed at the bottom of the list can only too easily be reduced to "propaganda"; points 5–8 in isolation can be translated into a fresh wave of Soviet rhetoric, and so forth. Point 10 is seldom cited by Western commentators, and when it is, it is to suggest that points 1–9 conflict with any residual Marxism the Soviet Union may espouse.

In other words, there are many possible interpretations, but they generally tend to the notion that as part of the process of de-ideologization of the USSR, "new thinking" is neither Marxism nor Marxism-Leninism, and that it is also not a theory or philosophy of international relations. In short, in Western eyes "new thinking" has been found to have little to do with thinking, and is thus widely perceived as something of a euphemistic misnomer.

We suggest as a complement to these interpretations the addition of the Soviet regime's self-assessment. Such an approach is not a return to the Western cold war approach, in which Soviet "new thinking" is automatically treated as ideology-*cum*-Communism (i.e., the Sovietological response to Stalinist Marxism-Leninism), which with the passage of years has become increasingly irrelevant. Instead of perceiving it as an immutable set of dogmas of a secular religion extrapolated from Bolshevik pronouncements and writings, we propose to treat "new thinking" as a Marxist *social theory:* normative, changing, and changeable, and always with the understanding that "objective" and "value-free" theories are not possible. It is in this regard that our approach differs from much of mainstream American Sovietology, which is still based on an implied positivist distinction between *their* value-laden ideologies and *our* objective and value-free theories. The introduction of such an approach requires that certain epistemological and methodological adjustments be made. In their absence there would seem to be no room for a Marxologue-Sovietologist who claims to approach the USSR through its "new thinking," understood as a social theory.

"New thinking" then ceases to be a set of slogans, and the treatment of any of its principles in isolation from the others makes no sense. We propose to examine "new thinking" as an autonomous concept that has gradually detached itself from its link with perestroika (and for that matter with Gorbachev). "New thinking" is in our view not a foreign policy expedient to gain breathing space (*peredyshka*) for the Soviet reformists (see Meissner 1987: 3), nor is it "another tissue of disinformation . . . to dupe the naive abroad" (Wettig 1987a: 144). The ten principles alone offer the outline of a new Soviet doctrine ("Gorbachev doctrine") on international relations that accurately reflects the realism and reformism of the post-Brezhnev era. Unlike Meissner and Wettig, other German analysts believe that "new thinking" has the potential to develop into a "grand theory" (*Grosskonzeption*; Berner and Dahm 1987: 5). We believe that that stage has already been reached: that the ten principles elaborated by Soviet writers on "new thinking" in the last few years have already become translated into a new philosophy of the world based on a new perception and a new conceptualization of diminishing Soviet capabilities and roles. It may well be a desperate effort doomed to failure, though it can also be seen as the casting about by a crippled superpower for a new strategy and the testing of the conceptual "armament" to go with it. The linchpin of that arsenal continues to be a form of Marxism-Leninism, and that is duly acknowledged.

If such an interpretation is conceivable, then it is clear that enquiry into the meaning of "new thinking" is urgently required. In the absence of clarification, "new thinking" might well go the way of "peaceful coexistence" and "correlation of forces" to become yet another Soviet *terminus technicus* seriously misunderstood in the West. Already another of Gorbachev's neologisms—glasnost—tends to mislead as the *feeling* spreads that the meaning is self-evident! Translated as "openness," it conjures up the friendly images of an open Western society, whereas the more accurate translation of "publicity" or "public airing" suggests the use of information or inquiry by an otherwise closed authoritarian society for purposes that the leadership alone defines.*

*In political terms the common usage of "openness" accords to Gorbachev's advantage by making his policy sound familiar, safe, incipiently democratic. No single thing, as Stephen Rosenfeld points out, "may have softened his Western reception more than the uncritical spreading of this one definition of glasnost by the journalists and others" ("'Openness' or Just Hot Air?," *The Guardian*, 28 June 1987, p. 16).

Similarly, as Bialer (1987: 64) points out, "democracy" to Gorbachev carries a different meaning than the one traditionally associated with it in the West.* Among the concepts associated with "new thinking," "balance of interests," which has generally been accepted at face value, is also widely misunderstood.† In these circumstances, investigation of the meaning of "new thinking" on international relations is no mere academic exercise in semantics.

Having identified the ten associations of "new thinking" and documented their provenance and development, it remains to bring them into *Soviet* focus, to see them as, first, an ideology and a new Soviet doctrine of international relations (chapter 2); second, a form of Marxism or Marxism-Leninism (chapter 3); third, a theory of international relations (chapter 4); and fourth, a foreign policy guide for action (chapter 5). It is our thesis that "new thinking" is all four: an ideology, a form of Marxism, and a theory of international relations, with its utility residing in the ability to translate into a guide for action. Each of these facets of "new thinking" is important, and each helps in understanding the others.

Our case rests on the validity of our hypothesis that Soviet "new thinking" pertains to the ten principles enumerated above. To confirm this view we examine Soviet texts (listed in Appendix 1), particularly those by the chief protagonists of "new thinking" in the Soviet Union (see Appendix 3), whose location within the Soviet party/state apparatus can be seen by referring to the chart in Appendix 4. We have included a selection of Soviet cartoons from *Pravda* portraying the Soviet Union and the world in the era of "new thinking" (Appendix 5), which we believe help to support our interpretation. Thus we seek to fill gaps that many Western analysts have

*Bialer argues that what Gorbachev means by "democracy" is almost the opposite of its Western meaning. He envisages grass-roots democracy at the microsocietal level—free elections at the enterprise, primary party organization, and local soviet—but not at the macroinstitutional level, which includes state and party organs. As another commentator points out, "democratisation" of the interstices of the party would exclude non-members of the party. It would mean no more than a democratization of the rule of whites in South Africa, not affecting apartheid in any way and maintaining the policy of excluding black voters (Handleman 1987: 33).

†"Balance of interests," according to Sestanovich, means that some traditional Soviet interests can be sacrificed (1988: 6). For discussion of the Soviet meaning, see below (pp. 78–84).

left open or have overlooked, and we offer this study as a complement to their analyses and interpretations. In that sense we do no more than follow the advice of an American Sovietologist who resists the study of "new thinking" qua thinking: "It is important to advance hypotheses as best we can, in part so that we can recognize the relevant evidence when it does come in" (Snyder 1987/88: 131).

We will conclude with the proposition that "new thinking" represents a profound challenge to the Western social sciences, above all to the subdisciplines of international relations and Sovietology (see chapter 6). That it constitutes a considerable challenge to Western policymaking would seem to go without saying.

"New thinking" might be short-lived, as many Sovietologists predict, but then again it might not. In any case it is important enough to merit study if only because as a product of one of the superpowers, it will no doubt have a place in the history of ideas.

Chapter 2

"NEW THINKING" AS SOVIET IDEOLOGY AND A NEW SOVIET DOCTRINE OF INTERNATIONAL RELATIONS

Critique of the Traditional Approach to Soviet Ideology

It has long been Western practice to regard writings that originate in totalitarian or authoritarian societies as intellectually deficient. It is a judgment that in American criticism has been built upon a mix of national parochialism* and epistemological positivism/empiricism, on which much of American social science is based. The low esteem in which Soviet Marxism-Leninism has been held stems not merely from its normative approach (inevitable in a variant of Marxism), but also because it forms the basis of a state ideology. Its function has been seen as limited to that of a secular religion, a source of unremitting rhetoric and domestic rituals, and its main role

---

*In the field of international relations, for example, apart from such exceptions as Alker and Biersteker's listing of the Soviet approach in their radical dialectical paradigm (H. E. Alker and T. J. Biersteker, "The Dialectics of World Order: Notes for a Future Archeologist of International Savoir-Faire," *International Studies Quarterly* 28 [1984]), criticism of the "omission" (e.g., V. Kubálková and A. A. Cruickshank, "A Double Omission," *British Journal of International Studies* 3, 3 [1977]) of Soviet theories from the concerns of international relations studies has gone unheeded. Even Stanley Hoffman, one of the first Americans to criticize explicitly the parochialism in the American international relations scene, excused the neglect of international studies of countries like the Soviet Union and China in which, as he put it, it would be hard to speak of free social science and scholarship ("An American Social Science: International Relations," *Daedalus* 106, 3 [Summer 1977]: 48). The Britisher Michael Banks took a different tack when he simply pronounced Soviet writing to be intellectually inferior—unfortunately omitting in the pronouncement any indication as to his yardstick ("The Inter-Paradigm Debate," in *International Relations: A Handbook of Current Theory*, eds. M. Light and A. J. R. Groom (London: Frances Pinter, 1984).

is perceived to lie in its legitimization of the rule of the Communist Party, in the indoctrination and political socialization of Soviet citizens, and in the rationalization of Soviet foreign policy. With any real thinking assumed to be paranoically disguised by a secretive, authoritarian regime, the writing originating from that regime was regarded by very few in the West (whether Sovietologist, Western Marxist, philosopher, international relations theorist, or policymaker) as a source of Soviet thinking or as thinking at all—in terms either of the revelation of Soviet intentions or of a heuristic contribution to our understanding of the world. The unravelling of Soviet writings has thus become the special preserve of Western pundits, Sovietologists, and foreign policy experts who claim to have the ability and acumen required to interpret Soviet thought and thought processes, while international relations theorists (British and American, for the most part) have taken responsibility for explaining the complexities of world politics for humanity as a whole. This approach, which reflected the somewhat parochial intellectual climate in the West during the cold war, has persisted, albeit for different reasons. During the optimistic years of detente, any inquiry into Soviet foreign policy that suggested that it was driven by its own (which is to say, different) Marxist-Leninist thinking was associated in many Western minds with a return to the conservative attitudes of the cold war. The notion of an "evil empire," with its implications of a "master plan" for world conquest, or that the Soviet Union and the West might have irreconcilably different ideologies, has been frowned upon and even ridiculed by American academia (cf. Dallin 1986).

There is, then, little or no tradition of serious Western study of Soviet thinking as thinking, and this is particularly true of the United States. If there were such a tradition, surely a series of analyses of the meaning of "new thinking" would have appeared to match the flood of Western writing on other aspects of Soviet reforms.* In these circumstances, in which direction are we to turn when the Russians force the issue by continuing to advance these far from intellectually deficient concepts of "new thinking," "new political thinking," and

---

*Few of the authors who in the past have written about Soviet ideology (e.g., V. Aspaturian, W. Zimmermann, Judson Mitchell, W. Griffith, J. F. Triska) have evaluated Soviet "new thinking" as thinking. The work of some who have done so (Glickham, Dallin, and Valkenier; in Germany, Meissner, Wettig, and Berner and Dahm; in the UK, Light and Shenfield) are referred to in this study.

even "new philosophy of international relations"? Do we say with those who have previously dismissed them that they are simply exaggerations, mere figures of Soviet speech, and continue with the customary Sovietological approach to the appraisal of Soviet writings?* Are we to proceed in our search of Soviet actions to discover if there is anything new in Soviet thinking, or do we assume that when the Soviets talk of "new thinking," it simply means that they are beginning to approximate *our* thinking—that Soviet "new thinking" has neither independent value nor autonomy nor intrinsic theoretical or political merit.

Soviet Ideology as the Core of the Soviet System

We take the position that Soviet "new thinking" should not be granted immunity from scholarly evaluation, but on the contrary should be analyzed as one of the *prime indicators* of real change in the USSR—a progress traditionally measured in the Western mind by the Soviet handling of human rights.[†]

We base our argument on the historical fact that it was the adoption of a "different" mode of thinking in 1917—Marxism-Leninism—that brought about the transformation of Russia from one of a states-system family of great powers into an anti-systemic Marxist-Leninist superpower and a near intractable element in international relations. The Soviet Union has always boasted of its ability to "think differently," and has never denied that the foundation of its thought is an ideology. In the Marxist tradition of treating *all* knowledge as

---

*For example, the interpretation of "new thinking" by Meissner and Wettig (i.e., as "another tissue of deception and disinformation, intended to dupe the naive abroad," "a mere temporary device, a defensive tactic while Gorbachev has domestic difficulties," "a new instance of Leninist peredyshka") is in the opinion of Alexander Dallin based on "a thoroughly mistaken view." Dallin admits that the Meissner and Wettig interpretation cannot be "disproven to everyone's satisfaction," indeed that it is "impossible to falsify," but as evidence he cites, first, a consensus of Sovietologists sharing his view; second, Soviet sources (e.g., Primakov [1987], who explicitly distances current thinking from the "breathing space" tradition); and third, a mix of "explicit . . . statements . . . by Soviet academics and practitioners" (Dallin 1987: 20, 21, 26, 6). Legvold similarly never reveals the basis of his judgment that certain Soviet pronouncements (and not others) "are more than just words" (1988: 10).

[†]Cf. R. Conquest in Dallin and Rice (1986).

socially produced, the Soviets insist that Western scholarship is part of the "bourgeois ideology of capitalism" inasmuch as in expressing views on society it necessarily reflects the interests of the ruling class. Since its inception, ideology has been for the Soviet Union what democratic processes and elections are for Western democracies, or what the filial relation is for monarchies. The Soviet political system continues to base its legitimacy on claims to a superior ideology; it is ruled by a working class party, in sharp contrast to the private property base of an (alienated) capitalist society. At the root of the system, then, is a superior type of *thinking* of which Marx thought only the proletariat (and Lenin, the proletariat under the guidance of the bolsheviks) is capable. Gorbachev can try to improve the thinking in that society, but he can never allow glasnost's concomitant of domestic pluralism to bring into question the leading role of the Communist Party. The moment the Communist Party abdicates its epistemologically privileged position, and therefore superior understanding of the world, from which alone springs its alleged capability of charting the course of humanity's development, will be the moment of system metamorphosis. There is as yet no evidence of such a transformation. Admission of the need to improve thinking within the Communist Party is a far cry from admission of inability to continue its constitutionally authorized leading role. Neither a reform that strengthens the office of President of the USSR nor the transfer of the country's day-to-day governance from the Party to a permanent legislature and local bodies (soviets) threatens the "leading role of the Communist Party in Soviet society." Rather it strengthens the leadership of Gorbachev, who as President of the USSR will still retain his job as General Secretary of the CPSU.*

*According to the constitutional changes adopted in November 1988 (to take effect in Spring 1989), both the new president and the new parliament will be elected by a 2,250-member "Congress of People's Deputies." Gorbachev's future as leader will no longer depend only on the support of the Politburo, with 12 voting members, and the Central Committee, with 251 (as of 25 April 1989) voting members—that is, on the two non-democratically constituted bodies that are picked from among delegates of the Party Congress. The Congress is theoretically the highest Party body; it meets every five years, and consists of delegates elected by party organizations from around the country. Party membership is not open to all, and with around 20 million members, it represents only one in eight adult Soviet citizens. With no reform of the single party system contemplated, even with multiple candidate contests, the degree of democracy in the new system might be challenged. The streamlined bicameral Supreme Soviet, which will have

In our view, an understanding of Soviet ideology has always been essential to an understanding of Soviet society. Additionally we believe Soviet writings have always contained coded statements of Soviet intentions, and afford crucial insights into the Soviet understanding of the world. No matter how skewed their world-view might be, with or without the addition of "new thinking," it is the world-view of a global superpower and, if for no other reason, constitutes an important part of world politics.

The Structure of Soviet Ideology

Toward the end of arriving at better understanding, we have argued that Soviet ideology should be viewed neither as amorphous nor homogeneous, but as consisting of a highly structured body of ideas whose various roles accord with their overall position within the ideological framework. It is a framework that can be represented in pyramidal form, with the ideas arranged on different levels of the pyramid (Kubálkova and Cruickshank 1985, 1989: 71ff). The ideas at the apex have always performed a largely rhetorical, propaganda, and legitimizing role while also acting as a binding agent of the whole Soviet system—a function unchanged throughout Soviet history. But the pyramid has other levels with other roles. The heuristic role of the pyramid's lower levels increases as these levels decline in axiomatic content and multiply the variables open to debate and to research. It is on these lower levels that scholarship comparable to Western theories of development, of anthropology, and so on are found. International relations, dealing with central questions such as war and peace, international conflict and cooperation, which touch generally on issues high up in the pyramid, has consistently been a very sensitive area politically, with narrower margins for debate than in other areas.

When Soviet thinking is viewed as a structured body of ideas, each performing a different function, it is clearly erroneous to treat all of it as "rhetoric," "propaganda," and the like. There have always

only 450 members instead of some 1,500, will differ from its predecessor inasmuch as its members will be chosen not in direct but in indirect elections, and it will be a full-time legislature with Communist Party members guaranteed one-third of the seats.

existed degrees of mobility and flexibility in the pyramidal structure, with old axioms opened to debate, or with ideas developed in relatively unconstrained research percolating upward. This is not to deny that in the past such change in either direction was a rare and often painful process. For significant change to be effected, one had to await the next Party Congress, when there might occur one of those rare periods of commotion in the ideology which resulted in rearrangement of the intellectual parameters for the whole of Soviet society. Nor is it to deny that scholarship at the lower levels was always tightly constrained, held in check by clusters of axioms not open for discussion, and carried out at serious personal risk by those who did not comply. Real, original research could take place only in the lacunae and in the elaboration of the axioms.

In these circumstances there has evolved a peculiar type of scholarship in the USSR that differs substantially from Western scholarship in its rationale and its methodology. The rationale of research in Western academia is to all intents and purposes the search for truth, using the best approach and employing the best methodology as designated on the basis of the reigning (in the past, often positivist) epistemological rules by a consensus of the academic community, and identified with the work of one or several members of that community. Thomas Kuhn caricatured the work of Western academia somewhat in his perhaps distortive concepts of "paradigms" and "paradigmatic exemplars"—that which approximates "research program" in Imre Lakatos's theory of knowledge. The research program sets positive as well as negative heuristic goals—that is to say, determines that which is sufficiently important to warrant study and that which is not. The "mainstream" approach is then taught, often against the backdrop of the others over which it has prevailed. It is analyzed, discussed, developed, and applied—and in turn demolished, in that endless search for truth that is the purpose of the Western intellectual system.

A very different rationale and set of rules have evolved in relation to Soviet scholarship. To begin with, there is no search for truth. Truth has already been revealed in Marxist-Leninist historical materialism and propounded in a series of axioms—for example, that the future of mankind is communism, that the socialist system alone, led by a Marxist-Leninist Communist Party, is locked onto the one true course, that the capitalist system is historically incapable of charting that course, and so forth. In all of this the academic community works within one axiomatically given paradigm, with discussion confined to approved side issues—never on primary goals or final ends.

The status and composition of the Soviet academy, both in an intellectual and a political sense, is also very different from its Western counterpart. The Marxian dictum of the "unity of theory and practice" not only denies academic freedom and academic autonomy, but also institutionalizes political interference by the Party in matters held sacrosanct by academics in the West. Thus the contours of the approved paradigm, as well as the identities of the paradigmatic exemplars, are defined by Party ideologues and policymakers in accordance with their own non-academic, non-scholarly criteria. Translated into a Western milieu, this would produce the absurd situation of chairmen of political science departments of prestigious universities summoned to the White House for the announcement of the latest "official" paradigm along with a list of its positive and negative "heuristics." In the president's office, textbooks on political science would be compiled, setting forth guidelines for political research by professional associations. The president would also pronounce on the curricula and reading lists of political science courses and oversee the selection of topics securely within the parameters of the approved paradigm.

Something like this has been the fate of Soviet scholarship. A monolithic ideology is a sine qua non of the "classless society," and the academic community, guided by political leaders, collaborates on the articulation of the one approved paradigm. This is one reason why those in the West who seek clarification are likely to continue to fail to find a clear Soviet statement on "new thinking." Judging from Western experience, it is usually its critics and not its champions who provide the most lucid statement of a paradigm;* in the Soviet Union there is no critique of or alternative paradigm to "new thinking," nor is a defense of "old thinking" offered.

Soviet scholarship has evolved different rules of procedure and criteria of judgment. Traditionally the goal has been persuasiveness in the presentation of points set forth in Party decrees. Scholarship

*For lucid summaries of power realism by its critics, see J. Vasquez, *The Power of Power Politics* (London: Frances Pinter, 1983); R. O. Keohane, ed., *Neorealism and Its Critics* (New York: Columbia University Press, 1986).

has been evaluated on the basis of the exposition, and on the discovery of new evidence in support of established doctrines. Such evidence is gathered from an approved list of Marxist classics and from speeches by the political leadership of the day. References to the work of fellow academics are rare. The limits within which axioms have been open for discussion, especially in the field of international relations, were too narrow to permit any real debate within the community of scholars. As a result, the massive output of thousands of books and journal articles on international relations from hundreds of Soviet and East European universities, academies, and institutes has been monotonous, repetitive, and often banal.

When it came to Soviet appraisal of Western scholarship, however, the situation was very different. Then it became a matter not only of dealing with another paradigm, but also of combatting a hostile ideology. Even in the period of "peaceful coexistence" (or detente, in Western eyes), when political, military, and economic forms of "class struggle" were relaxed, the constant of ideological confrontation remained and, if anything, was intensified. Accordingly, the demolition of "bourgeois" ideas and theories was pursued without remission.

As it happened, the attacks by Soviet scholars elicited no reply from their Western counterparts. Kept at a distance, Soviet scholars could only follow in frustration the convolutions of Western debates on international relations. To the Soviet critics, none of the approaches suggested in the Western debates commended itself; ideologically all were of the same ilk, and consequently were dismissed. The Soviet interest in Western debates was not to learn, but to demonstrate the validity of the Soviet approach. It is hardly surprising, then, that Soviet critiques of Western scholarship have consistently failed to attract attention in the West, even when they are available in translation.

"New Thinking" and Soviet Ideology

How much has the approach of Soviet scholarship changed under Gorbachev? Are the optimistic interpretations by some commentators on Gorbachev's USSR correct, and is there indeed some indication of the abandonment of the ideological axioms of commitment to communism, class struggle, etc.—e.g., by the deliberate collapsing of the ideological pyramid onto its base, or by the detachment of the apex and its distancing from real thinking, making the axioms irrelevant?

To date there is little evidence of such change. Indeed the "new thinking" neither contradicts nor runs counter to established practice: "new thinking" is still no more than a new Soviet state ideology officially promulgated by Gorbachev that sets new axioms and parameters for Soviet intellectual discourse. However, it cannot be said that no change has taken place: there are significant differences that suggest that "new thinking" will inform a rather different ideology, albeit one still pyramidal in form, defined by the hierarchy of its levels and sacrosanct axioms. We see significant differences both in the provenance of the new axioms and in the greater freedom of debate they afford within the Soviet Union and in its relations with the outside world. In exploring these differences, we look first at the circumstances in which "new thinking" was enunciated and then at its sources.

Gorbachev's Political Report to the 27th Congress

It is a fact to which attention is seldom drawn that it was at the 27th Congress of the CPSU (1986) that all the main principles of "new thinking" we identified above (p. 6) were promulgated and adopted by the Congress as the Soviet state ideology.* The search by Western authors through the pages of *Pravda, Kommunist,* and other journals for the original sources of "new thinking" seems quite unnecessary.

"New thinking" was not announced as items of an agenda, nor were its principles elaborated at the Congress. It was embodied in occasional phrases or sentences, unobtrusively inserted in Gorbachev's five-hour speech,† which were overlooked by many com-

*For a detailed textual analysis of Gorbachev's political report and comparison with the resolutions adopted by the Congress, as well as with the political report made by Brezhnev at the previous CPSU Congress, see Glickham (1986).

†Battle (1988: 576) draws attention to similar "hidden" phrases in the political report in regard to changes of electoral procedures, which by foreshadowing them made them possible. Peterson and Trulock point to "a carefully managed, public reformulation of national security objectives and policies . . . [b]eginning at the 27th Party Congress in February 1986 and continuing for well over a year" based on the concept of "reasonable sufficiency" mentioned in the report (1988: 18–19).

mentators who argued that not much new had come out of the Congress (Mastny 1987: 6). A comparison of Gorbachev's report with that of Brezhnev five years before reveals that, although the world views they projected had much in common, the two leaders diverged sharply in their evaluation of some central postulates of Soviet foreign policy (Glickham 1986: 8). The crucial point for our study is that all the key words and phrases of "new thinking" appeared in Gorbachev's report. For the time being they were not debated, and they gradually emerged as ideological parameters through a steadily increasing flow of references in newspaper columns, journal articles, books and their titles, and public addresses.

In his political report, Gorbachev did not use the expression "new thinking," favoring instead "rethinking" and "new approach," but "new thinking" was soon to become inextricably linked with the definition as "a break with the way of thinking and acting that for centuries has been built on the acceptability, the permissibility, of wars and armed conflict" (1986a: 28).* He used both "new approaches" and "new thinking" prior to the Congress, and before he became General Secretary of the CPSU, as early as 18 December 1984, when, in an address to British parliamentarians, he declared that "the nuclear age inevitably demands new political thinking" (1987c, 2: 112). The first occasion on which he used the expression "new political thinking" *after* he became General Secretary was prior to the 27th Congress (15 January 1986) in a statement proposing the complete elimination of nuclear weapons.

The principles of "new thinking" mentioned in Gorbachev's political report to the Congress were elaborated more fully in his speech at the rally commemorating the seventieth anniversary of the October Revolution. He also spelled out the ten points in his book *Perestroika and New Thinking* (1987). On each of these occasions, in his capacity as General Secretary, Gorbachev took the opportunity to set his seal on the new axioms.

As Glickham (1986: 5) points out, the final resolution of the Congress did not actually use the term *global*, but the global thrust

---

*"A turning point has arisen not only in internal but also in external affairs. The changes in the development of the contemporary world are so profound and significant that they require a rethinking and comprehensive analysis of all its factors. The situation of nuclear confrontation calls for new approaches, methods, and forms of relations between different social systems, states and regions" (Gorbachev 1986a: 4).

was there, as were all ten associated points, albeit in the guise of key words, key phrases, or even slogans. Some are also included in the new edition of the CPSU program that was adopted after revision to bring it into line with the spirit of "new thinking." The program defines the Party's long-term domestic and foreign policy goals, which are also the goals of the Soviet state. It is within this framework that policy in general, based on the General Secretary's political report, is finalized by the Congress and the medium-term policy of the state is fixed in legally binding terms.

Thus, in both Gorbachev's political report and the new edition of the CPSU program, we find references to ecological problems, to world poverty, and to global nuclear problems (1986a: 10), to the threat posed by these having created an "interdependence" of "states and people" (4) (our points #1 and #2), and to the imperative need to make the break from pre-nuclear age thinking that regarded armed conflict as acceptable (28). Significantly the Party program goes on to refer to the "interests of mankind to be reconciled optimally with those of states and nations"; the overall global thrust of these concerns is echoed in references to the "world community" in Gorbachev's political report. None of this is to be found in Brezhnev's political report to the previous Congress.

Gorbachev's report cites our point #3—namely, the need for renunciation of war in favor of peaceful coexistence. In his report the meaning of peaceful coexistence has already changed with the dropping of references to peaceful coexistence as a form of class struggle. Although the party program insists that "peaceful coexistence . . . is not simply the absence of war . . . but an international order" (CPSU 1986: 7), Gorbachev's use of "peace" comes closer than ever before to its Western definition as the "absence of hostilities" and the "opposite of war." In these circumstances, with peace elevated to the "highest human value," Gorbachev insists that the notion of "Soviet threat" must be without foundation. He refers also to the indivisibility of security (our point #4). The Party program refers to a "comprehensive and reliable system of security . . . to embrace the whole world." Gorbachev identifies "international economic security" as one of the pillars of a global security system, whose achievement has become a political, not a military, task (1986a: 27) (our point #6). He also proffers the theoretically intriguing notion (soon to be cited by the Soviet academic community as "new thinking's" major contribution to theory) that the goal in international relations should be a "balance of interests" (28). The "level of military confrontation in all areas" (28) is to be reduced (our point #7), with military parity (still described as a "historic achievement" in the program) no longer seen as capable of serving as a guarantee of deterrence. The strategic objective is to be the achievement of "reliable security" (29) (cf. "reasonable sufficiency" in our point #8). Both documents stress the need to lower the level of military confrontation. On this subject the Party program refers to the elimination of nuclear weapons and other weapons of mass destruction, the avoidance of the militarization of outer space, and the dismantling of military bases, which it commends to the particular attention of the permanent members of the UN Security Council. The stress on flexibility in international relations (our point #9) that infuses both the new edition of the Party program and Gorbachev's report suggests a much more realistic assessment of the world and a reappraisal of capitalism—the USSR's main adversary—and its life expectancy. It dispels the erstwhile confident belief in the advance of the Soviet Union and its entourage of socialist countries on the path to communism. The rationale for adopting a "new edition" of an existing program, instead of a new program, reflects in some measure the "new thinking's" restrained realism.

Finally, there is little room for doubt about the validity of our point #10—namely, the continuing commitment of the USSR to Marxism-Leninism. The emphasis in both Gorbachev's report and the Party program on the need for theoretical Marxist-Leninist understanding and the "new approaches" cannot be gainsaid. The report attempts to pinpoint the cause of humanity's present predicament by asserting that the scientific-technological revolution generated largely by capitalism has produced a destructive capacity which capitalism cannot by itself contain. Gorbachev continues to adhere to the ideological blueprint of two conflicting worlds—socialist and capitalist—but depicts them now as coexisting in the context of one interrelated and interdependent planet. The mode of thought that continues to distinguish socialism from capitalism is Marxist-Leninist historical materialism based on dialectics—a concept repeatedly stressed by Gorbachev in his book *Perestroika*.

The Sources of "New Thinking"

If the choice of Party Congress as the venue for the change of state ideology echoed past scenarios and followed time-honored patterns, it is not to say that there have not been important departures from established practice in other respects. One of these departures has to do with the various sources of "new thinking," which include not only earlier Soviet doctrines (the Soviets stress continuity with their past), but also a number of Soviet theoretical constructs developed in the lower levels of the "ideological pyramid" in the 1970s and 1980s, or even earlier. A truly novel aspect of "new thinking" (and obviously intentional) is the dual nature of its sources. Hence we find that Soviet sources anticipating "new thinking" parallel and even paraphrase Western sources. "New thinking" is not the brainchild of Gorbachev. It is no more the spontaneous product of any one mind than it is a set of untried measures hastily put together to redress a serious domestic crisis. As a glance at the background and sources will indicate, it is not an "afterthought"—less important to the recovery and progress of the Soviet system than either perestroika or glasnost: it is a carefully considered logical progression from earlier Soviet ideological and intellectual development. As Glickham (1986: 10) points out, "new thinking" has a history and a constituency both in Soviet academic circles and in the Party apparatus. What Glickham fails to point out, however, is that "new thinking" also has a long history and a significant constituency *in the West*. This is the genuinely novel aspect of "new thinking."

(1): Khrushchev's Doctrine of Peaceful Coexistence

Although the rigidity of earlier Soviet foreign policy, particularly that of Brezhnev, is openly renounced in "new thinking," the overall continuity with earlier Soviet policy and doctrine is not denied. Says Primakov:

The continuity of the Soviet state's foreign policy line is of course indisputable. But all the same, at present qualitatively new conditions . . . make it necessary—perhaps more insistently necessary than at any earlier time in our history—to treat a whole series of key problems of international life in an innovative way (1987: 1).

There is in fact no body of Soviet ideas about international relations, identifiable as "old thinking," for which "new thinking" is a replacement, which has led some to conclude incorrectly that it is simply the rigidity of Gorbachev's predecessors that is being rejected. The obverse side of the "new thinking" coin must be sought elsewhere. The place of Khrushchev in the genealogy of "new thinking" merits attention if only because of Gorbachev's failure to acknowledge him. It was, after all, against the backdrop of Khrushchev's doctrine of peaceful coexistence that Brezhnev's "rigid" foreign policies and "theoretical" innovations were conceived.*

It might be argued that the danger of nuclear conflict was appreciated by Soviet leaders as far back as Malenkov. However, instead of acknowledging Malenkov or Khrushchev, Gorbachev appends his doctrine to Lenin's version of peaceful coexistence. Yet the continuity of "new thinking" with the 1956 Khrushchev doctrine is unmistakable despite a thirty-year interval. The doctrine that emerged from the 27th CPSU Congress is that enunciated at the 20th Congress writ large. The reluctance to acknowledge Khrushchev (as a Soviet writer admits) can readily be understood because of Khrushchev's incautious, sometimes threatening remarks ("We will bury you"), from which any "new thinking" that depends on eliminating the image of Soviet threat has to be dissociated (Antonovich, in "Perestroika" 1988: 13). In this study, however, we shall attempt to show that, as a theory of international relations, the departure of Gorbachev's "new thinking" from Khrushchev's peaceful coexistence is less radical than its departure from Lenin's theory of imperialism.

The "qualitatively new conditions" that Primakov refers to have lifted the cloud over the principle of "technological determinism," which thirty years ago, at the time of the enunciation of Khrushchev's doctrine of peaceful coexistence, was seen as "heretical." The lapse of time is not surprising because until recently, in many Western Marxist minds, technological determinism was

*The two major theoretical innovations attributed to Brezhnev are, first, the "Brezhnev Doctrine," which can be seen as a restatement of "socialist internationalism," and for which Brezhnev should not take exclusive credit (Kubálková and Cruickshank 1985: 89), and, second, his notion of "developed socialism" as a description of the stage reached by the Soviet Union during his period in office. Gorbachev's program of perestroika and open recognition of "underdeveloped socialism" in the USSR belies any theory of developed socialism, but so far the Brezhnev Doctrine has not been officially repudiated.

viewed as apostasy.* Before the advent of the "new thinking," Soviet writers discussing peaceful coexistence have sought to avoid sounding too "revisionist," and have denied what has become "new thinking's" major premise—namely, that doctrinal change (in this case, "new thinking" itself) is a result of the development of atomic weapons. So it happens that, notwithstanding the technological determinist implications, many Soviet theoreticians now find corroboration in all the Marxist classics of the notion that each major development in science forces philosophy to change its form.†

It is interesting that the observation attributed to Khrushchev that the atomic bomb does not observe the class principle has been reiterated thirty years later by Gorbachev. The technological realities have prevailed and led to a full endorsement of Khrushchev's beliefs that the bomb would kill more of the progressive "sheep" than of the imperialist "goats" because of the larger total number of sheep. Gorbachev goes further: humanity has lost its immortality, and the survival of the species is now very much on the line. Since technological determinism was ideologically unacceptable justification in 1956, the official rationale for the adoption of the doctrine of peaceful coexistence was found in the "changed correlation of forces"—a change deriving essentially from the inclusion of the decolonized Third World in the "zone of peace." If the Third World was combined with the socialist bloc, then in the competition between socialism and capitalism, it was no longer clear who could be said to be encircling whom. The doctrine of "socialism in one country" that had previously governed the direction of foreign policy was formally

*For Western Marxist parallels, see the debate that followed British historian E. P. Thompson's coining the term *exterminism* to denote the "last stage of civilization," characterized by an irrational arms race that has obliterated socioeconomic differences between the United States and the USSR. Thompson expresses doubts at the theoretical capacity of Marxist historical materialism to come to grips with the problems of the nuclear age ("Notes on Exterminism, the Last Stage of Civilization," *New Left Review* 121 [1980] and Thompson et al., *Exterminism and the Cold War* [London: Verso, 1982]. See also Kubálková and Cruickshank [1985: 18, 217, 230, 237, 341–43; 1986]). Raymond Williams rejected the concept of exterminism precisely on the grounds of its derivation from technological determinism.

†The Marxist classics are cited for saying that, with each technological change, theory also needs to change (e.g., Mshvenieradze [1986: 51] and Yakovlev [1987: 18] cite Engels, while Plimak [1987: 73, 86] cites both Marx and Lenin).

repudiated, and the strength of the "progressive forces" assessed by the optimistic, certainly premature, gauging of the correlation of forces (half of mankind was on the side of the USSR) made global war and nuclear war between socialism and capitalism (as well as regional wars that might develop into global war) *no longer inevitable.* Although not entirely repudiated, war was considered not only no longer inevitable but indeed undesirable. The peaceful coexistence principle was to apply to relations between socialist and capitalist states only to prevent clashes on a global scale with nuclear weapons (or regional conflicts that might lead to involvement by the nuclear powers). War was not renounced in other areas, however. Wars of national liberation, for example, enjoyed the holy status of *jihad*, and as such might be waged behind the nuclear shield of peaceful coexistence.

Another aspect of the coexistence doctrine that anticipated Soviet "new thinking" thirty years later was the possibility of economic and political cooperation between the United States and the USSR; this was to become a fundamental principle of detente in the 1970s, and it now finds expression in the Soviet concept of "interdependence within one global economy." Ever since the original enunciation of the doctrine, much has been made of the unrelenting ideological struggle, in which no relaxation has ever been countenanced. After all, "peaceful coexistence of states of different socio-economic systems" was first and foremost a form of class struggle. If in certain circumstances, a lessening in intensity of the class struggle in its political, military, and economic forms had become conceivable, in the remaining ideological sphere it must be waged without remission. The concept of peaceful coexistence of states as a form of class struggle has now been abandoned,* but we are assured that ideological confrontation will continue in a different form with more sophisticated "weapons."

(2): Recent Soviet and Western Sources

The genealogy of Gorbachev's concept of "new thinking" can be seen as a logical progression from earlier Soviet doctrines. The main innovative elements appear to be, first of all, that many of its

---

*See chapter 3 below, p. 71.

concepts are ideas picked up by Gorbachev and his advisors from the margins of Soviet academic writing, where they have been languishing for over a decade, and second, that many have clear parallels in, if not explicit derivations from, Western sources. These derivations are, significantly, not disputed by Soviet writers. Plimak, for example, documenting the Western sources of "new thinking," puts them in "thousands and thousands of books and articles" (1987: 74), thereby repudiating another traditional axiom of Soviet ideology: the prohibition against drawing on Western sources, or even studying them.

Although Soviet physicist and dissident Andrei Sakharov (fully reinstated in the Gorbachev period), in his famous 1968 essay *Progress, Coexistence, and Intellectual Freedom*, warns of the threat to humanity in the nuclear age, the main credit for issuing the warning has gone to a Westerner. Since 1986 Soviet writers have openly attributed the expression "new thinking" to Albert Einstein, who called for it shortly after the advent of atomic weapons in 1945, thereby giving additional substantiation (in the Soviet view) to the Marx-Engels dictum that with each change in the natural sciences, philosophy must also change in form. In his political report, Gorbachev returns frequently to Einstein's phrase "the time demands new thinking," but without specific acknowledgment. However, with no apparent qualms, other Soviet writers before and after Gorbachev acknowledge Einstein (e.g., Bovin 1986b, 1988; Frolov 1986; Petrovsky 1986; Arbatov 1987; Plimak 1987; Shevardnadze 1988). His call for "new thinking" was repeated in the Einstein-Russell manifesto of 1955 that inaugurated the Pugwash peace movement of Western scientists. Oddly enough, most (if not all) Western enquiries into the roots of "new thinking" fail to mention the Soviets' attribution of the term to a Westerner. Yet Soviet awareness of the notion of "thinking new" in the nuclear age was long established, with a 1977 article commemorating the origins of the Pugwash movement (entitled "Have We Learned to Think New?") appearing almost a decade before Soviet ideology adopted the Einstein phrase (Markov 1977).

The associated principles of "new thinking" also have a history in both Soviet and Western writings. The Soviets refer to the long (indeed pre-revolutionary) Russian tradition of pacifism, and to the work of Lev Tolstoy in particular. The notion of "global" problems goes back in the Soviet Union at least ten years.* In 1984 Gromyko and Lomeiko (the former a son of Andrei Gromyko) published a book entitled *Novoe myshlenie v iadernyi vek* [New thinking in the nuclear age] which so fascinated Soviet readers that it sold 100,000 copies in one week (*Washington Post*, 5 January 1986). In the same book Gromyko and Lomeiko discuss interdependence, referring to it with some hesitation as a "Western concept," but not according it the prominent place it has since come to occupy. The concept of "all-human" morality too, and its identification with (if not substitution for) "communist" morality, and generally the subordination of the "class" approach to the "all-human" has an even longer history in Soviet writing.[†]

Apart from the discussion in Soviet writing of the various parts of what was to become "new thinking," there were a number of articles published before Gorbachev's enunciation of the concept at the 27th CPSU Congress, directly foreshadowing "new thinking" in all its aspects (e.g., an article by Primakov in *Pravda*, 22 January 1986). In our view the most prescient as an introduction to "new thinking" was "The Logic of Political Thinking in the Nuclear Era," by Georgi Shakhnazarov (1984), published some three months before the book by Gromyko and Lomeiko. Except for the concept of flexibility in international relations and the notion of "reasonable sufficiency," all aspects of "new thinking" are covered in Shakhnazarov's article. The observation (made by Glickham) that some of his points have a tentative flavor does not in our view detract from Shakhnazarov's anticipation of "new thinking" as a package.

Shakhnazarov asserts the priority of international over national problems, and anticipates much of current Soviet analysis by insisting

---

*See D. Gvishiani, "Global Problems and Global Modelling," *MEMO*, 1979/3; E. Fedorov, "Globalnye problemy sovremennosti i razoruzhenie," *MEMO*, 1979/1; V. Zagladin and I. T. Frolov, *Globalnye problemy sovremennosti, nauchnye i sotsialnye aspekty* (Moscow, 1981). In September 1983 G. L. Smirnov (then Director of the USSR Academy of Sciences' Institute of Philosophy) noted the tremendous impact of global problems on the fate of mankind ("Za reshitelnyi povorot filosofskikh issledovanii k sotsialnoi praktike," *Voprosy filosofii* 9 [1983]).

[†]See P. M. Egides, *Smysl zhizni, v chom on?* [The purpose of life, where is it?] (Moscow, 1963); "Marksistskaya etika o smysle zhizni" [Marxist ethics about the purpose of life], *Voprosy filosofii* 8 (1963); G. D. Bandzeladze, ed., *Aktualnye problemy marksistskoj etiki* (Tbilisi, 1967); see also the entry *obshchechelovecheskoe* [all-human] in O. G. Drobnickoj and I. S. Kon, eds., *Kratkij slovar po etike* [Short dictionary of ethics] (Moscow, 1965).

that there is no contradiction between global and class problems (1984: 67, 72). He describes the end of "national egoism" (68), giving way to a "world society" (*mirovoe soobshchestvo*) (67); he advocates renunciation of war (73) and ridicules the notion of Soviet threat (65); he asserts that peace and the survival of mankind is the highest human value (63), and argues that security is not attainable by military but only by political means (73); he expands on the need to reduce levels of military confrontation (66). He distinguishes between *doatomnoe myshlenie* (thinking of the pre-nuclear age) and "planetary or internationalist thinking" of the nuclear age—a distinction for which, together with the dictum to "think new," he gives credit to Russell and Einstein (64). He concludes with the observation that the shift from pre-nuclear to nuclear thinking now has to be accomplished faster: the technologically determined break between the nuclear and pre-nuclear age is not only greater than that between the thinking of Ptolemy, Copernicus, Newton, and Einstein, but it also threatens human civilization.

Clearly the assumption that "new thinking" is something new in the USSR—or in the West—is unwarranted. The salient feature is the Soviet readiness to acknowledge non-Marxist sources or parallels. This propensity is quite common in Western Marxism, where "lateral bourgeois influences" are regarded as almost as significant as Marx himself,* but it is so innovative a feature in Soviet writings that it has led some commentators to the conclusion that "new thinking" is no longer Marxist. In their attempts to lessen the impact of "bourgeois influences" by tracing "new thinking" to a Marxist root, Soviet writers remind us that the idea of the interdependence of socialism and capitalism derives from Lenin's understanding of the Soviet Union as "a part of the system of states" (Nikita Zagladin, in "Perestroika" 1988: 8). Similarly they note that the Einstein-Russell manifesto was initiated by Frederic Joliot-Curie, a leading member of the French Communist Party (Frolov 1986: 3–4). Conveniently, then, most of the principles of "new thinking" have dual sources—Soviet (or Marxist) and Western—either of which may be cited to fit changing circumstances.

---

*E.g., the influence of Croce on Gramsci, Weber on Lukacs, Freud, Schopenhauer, Nietzsche, Dilthey, and Bergson on the Frankfurt school, the French school of *Annales* on Wallerstein.

Apart from Einstein and Russell, the Western sources are Herman Kahn, Willy Brandt, Jonathan Schell, Niels Bohr, and Olaf Palme. Even the Pope and Catholic church come in for occasional favorable mention, as do resolutions adopted by the UN General Assembly (Plimak 1987: 74). Examples of "East-West" theoretical overlap with reference to our ten points of "new thinking" include the "radical salvationism" of Richard Falk and the American-based World Order Model Project (WOMP), which "new thinking" comprehends in points 1 and 4; the liberal theories of interdependence, which overlap point 2; a number of cosmopolitan normative theories of international relations, which duplicate points 3–4; and the principles of the various peace movements, which are echoed in point 3, with apologies to the movements for Lenin's contempt for pacifism, which is now perceived to have been misplaced.* The notion of Soviet threat is denied by Western Marxist or liberal theorists of the "New Cold War";† the ideas of Olaf Palme's commission surface in point 5; the work of the Club of Rome and Willy Brandt's North-South program for survival run parallel to point 1; and the notions of "nuclear winter" and accidental nuclear exchange are reflected in points 1–2, as are the concepts of exterminism and anti-nuclearism (referred to above). In other words, the description of the world that purports to be "new" approximates closely that of the Western peace movements, the radical liberals (or simply liberals), and the social democrats, with an overall Marxist gloss. In the Soviet literature listed in Appendix 1, there are long passages that seem to be lifted more or less verbatim from Western sources.

This, then, is certainly a new feature of Soviet "new thinking": the attempt to extend its ideological reach beyond the USSR. The Soviet commentator is on target who enjoins us to see "New Thinking . . . as acceptable to both systems."** However, Soviet thinkers see a tutelary role for themselves vis-à-vis a capitalist system that

---

*See V. Zagladin, "Der Krieg lauft uberhaupt den Bestrebungen der Partei der Kommunisten zuwider," in *Probleme des Friedens und des Sozialismus* (Prague, 1987), pp. 588–96.

†See, for example, Fred Halliday, *The Making of the New Cold War* (London: Verso, 1983). For a discussion of this literature, see Kubálkova and Cruickshank, "The 'New Cold War' in 'Critical International Relations Studies,'" *Review of International Studies* 12, 13 (July 1986).

**"October Revolution, Peaceful Coexistence," *New Times*, 9 November 1987.

by itself is "incapable of 'new thinking'" (Bovin 1986: 120). Bovin allows that there are individuals in the capitalist world capable of "new thinking," and of uniting with fellow thinkers in the Soviet Union, but it is only to be expected that considerable resistance to "new thinking" should be encountered from the "old thinking" in the capitalist system. In that respect a Soviet critic singles out the German historians Meissner and Wettig for their inability to "think new" (Zagorsky 1988). Or a NATO general, having erred in Soviet eyes, is blamed for "not yet thinking new."*

The first nine points of "new thinking" are clearly intended to serve as the foundation of a new global ideology for Marxists and non-Marxists alike. There is a curious reversal here as the USSR casts itself in the role of fellow traveller of those who espouse these views, but the stress in both Soviet political documents and scholarly writings reaffirms the Soviets' continuing commitment to Marxism. Indeed both ideologue and scholar reiterate their perception of the world as based on the "given" that socialism and capitalism are two antagonistic modes of production coexisting side by side, with socialism based on the superior mode of thought—Marxism. Whether Marxism can handle the problems of the nuclear age, whether there is a "nuclear age," and whether or not it may respond to "new thinking" are not parts of "new thinking."

Whether they are foreign additions or neglected Soviet sources, there are various ways of incorporating them into Soviet Marxism-Leninism and a "new," radically modernized historical materialism. The process of developing ideologically acceptable terms involves a high order of thinking, and conceivably may open genuine debate in the USSR for the first time since the late 1920s. By the sharing of certain ideas with the West, the distance between Soviet and Western political discourse could be substantially narrowed to a point where the often casual Western dismissal of Soviet writings would be tantamount to a dismissal of their Western colleagues. Although many of the Western sources of "new thinking" are on the margins of Western scholarship, such views are usually not rejected by their mainstream colleagues without some scholarly evaluation.

TASS, 9 November 1988 (Moscow); FBIS, SOV-88-218, 10 November 1988.

"New Thinking" by Soviet New Thinkers

The thrust of our argument so far has been that "new thinking" is a "modernized" and "Westernized" state ideology which allows for a greater degree of "non-dogmatic" "creative" thought about its main elements. This argument is based on a review of recent Soviet writings and an awareness of intellectual relationships and patterns within the party and academic hierarchies. We submit that a scrutiny of the publications that deal with "new thinking"—their dominant themes, their relationship to each other and to the writings of Gorbachev, coupled with the names, and the political and intellectual profile of their authors, provides sufficient "circumstantial evidence" to reveal a pattern and allow informed guesses to be made as to the meaning of "new thinking," the point reached in its development, its status and "state of the art."

It seems evident that behind "new thinking" there was a time and a team. The time was a period of wide-ranging agreement (or at least compromise) in the collective leadership reached soon after Gorbachev's ascent to power in 1985. The area of agreement concerned the urgent need for a restructured doctrine of international relations to complement the domestic restructuring (perestroika). Some of the members of the team must already have known the direction in which the new doctrine would lead; without such knowledge the inclusion of certain "key words" and "key phrases" in Gorbachev's political report only a year after his election would have been very unlikely, as would the orchestration of the extensive media campaign of 1986 and 1987 to popularize the concept of "new thinking."

We turn now to the central "new thinking" figures who may be said to have been its architects. A number of Western commentators have observed that the changeover of personnel in international relations has been more radical than in any other area of Soviet leadership, and that the foreign policy team has undergone a complete changeover of staff. As most Western analyses of new Soviet foreign policy (to which "new thinking" has often been reduced) have shown, all major agencies involved in the formulation of foreign policy—Politburo, Ministry of Foreign Affairs, International Department of the Central Committee, Socialist Countries Department of the Central Committee—have been substantially restructured or newly created since Gorbachev became General Secretary (see Appendix 4). No less remarkable has been the changeover in the leadership of the chief agency dealing with ideology—the Ideological Commission of the Central Committee—and among those in charge of military planning in the Ministry of Defense. Top personnel responsible for the implementation of "economic interdependence" and the chiefs in the Ministry of Foreign Trade have been similarly dealt with.

Most of the new promotions have not been from within the relevant international relations or ideology apparatus, but from areas totally unrelated to either. The overall effect of such wholesale change casts some doubt on the accuracy of the widely held perception that foreign policy and its ideological foundations have only a secondary role (peredyshka) in Soviet calculations. This is bolstered by consideration of the placement and consolidation of leading new thinkers in strategic foreign policy and ideology positions.*

The officeholders in the top party positions in the fields of international relations and ideology include some of the most prominent spokesmen of "new thinking"; in addition to Gorbachev, there is Yakovlev, Dobrynin, Medvedev, and Shevardnadze. Yakovlev and Dobrynin in particular have published on "new thinking" in international relations at a rate of at least one article a year each. Stressing the need for new research to match "new thinking," Dobrynin's article in June 1986 in *Kommunist* was one of the earliest elaborations by a high-ranking Soviet party official to include all ten associated

---

*See Appendixes 3 and 4 below. The new agencies are the Commission on International Relations of the Central Committee, the Commission for Ideology, and the new *office* of the President of the USSR—all of which have significant roles in the field of foreign policy. The agencies in the foreign policy and ideology areas that have experienced significant changes of staff are (1) the Politburo, with Gorbachev succeeding Chernenko in March 1985, (2) the Ministry of Foreign Affairs, where Shevardnadze succeeded Gromyko in July 1985, (3) the Commission on International Policy of the Central Committee, headed by Aleksandr Yakovlev since formed in October 1988, (4) the International Department of the Central Committee, headed since October 1988 by Valentin Falin, (5) the Commission for Ideology of the Central Committee, headed since October 1988 by Vadim Medvedev, and (6) the substantially strengthened position of the President of the USSR, a role that Gorbachev has occupied since October 1988. The important institutional and personnel changes under Gorbachev include the disbanding of the Socialist Countries Department, headed for a long time by the Brezhnevite Konstantin Rusakov and, more recently, by Vadim Medvedev.

principles. With Dobrynin's semi-retirement and resignation from his position as Secretary of the Central Committee, followed by his transfer to a position in the Supreme Soviet as aide to Gorbachev, those who see Yakovlev, Gorbachev, and Shevardnadze as the most central figures in the development and implementation of "new thinking" at Central Committee and Politburo level are correct.

There are of course other party figures who have written at length on the subject—Primakov, for example. For many years director of the USSR Academy of Sciences' Institute of Oriental Studies, Primakov was promoted in December 1985 to head the Academy's Institute for World Economy and International Relations. A *Pravda* article by Primakov entitled "The Road to the Future" appeared in January 1986 (Primakov 1986b) as one of a series on significant elements of "new thinking," and, taken together with his inclusion in the team to Reykjavik (with Gorbachev, Dobrynin, Yakovlev, and Arbatov), it seemed to indicate that he already exerted considerable influence.* Ten days after the Party Congress Primakov spoke not of "new thinking" but of "a new philosophy of security," which seemed to suggest that the whole concept was still being given serious thought at the highest level. Further articles on "new thinking" followed, and one in particular entitled "A New Philosophy of Soviet Foreign Policy" (Primakov 1987a) made such an impression in the West (prominently displayed in English translation in the *Current Digest of the Soviet Press* under the title "A New 'Flexibility' in Soviet Foreign Policy") that many Western commentators assumed it to be the source of "new thinking."

Among the most important contributors to the development of "new thinking" has been Georgi Shakhnazarov, whose advancement under Gorbachev was first drawn to Western attention by Archie Brown (cf. Brown 1986b: 72). If Yakovlev emerges as the strongest political supporter of Gorbachev's "new thinking," it is Shaknazarov whose influence at the highest intellectual level is paramount. For

---

*His long experience in the field of international relations and ideology includes his service as chairman of the Soviet Committee on the Defense of Peace (as of 1983), and vice-chairman of the Scientific Senate of the USSR on the Investigation of Peace and Disarmament Problems. Since 1986 he has also been a representative chairman of the World Peace Senate—a "front organization" directed by the International Division of the Central Committee of the Party Secretariat.

many years president of the Soviet Association of Political Sciences and vice-president of the International Political Sciences Association, Shaknazarov was formerly head of a sector at the Institute of State and Law of the Academy of Sciences in Moscow, and since the 1970s one of several deputy heads of the Socialist Countries Department of the Central Committee of the CPSU. In the summer of 1986, shortly after Medvedev became head of the Socialist Countries Department, Shaknazarov was promoted to first deputy head. The elevation of Medvedev to the top ideology position was accompanied by Shaknazarov's advance to the role of personal aide to Gorbachev, reinforcing the perception of his central role in the intellectual development of "new thinking." Besides his wide-ranging intellect and versatility (he has published a number of science-fiction novels under the pseudonym "Georgi Shakh"), Shakhnazarov has on several occasions demonstrated an ability to anticipate events and recommend courses of action and measures that in time have duly become official policy.* We have already noted this quality of prescience at work as early as 1984 and his "anticipation" then of many of "new thinking's" significant features. We come later to another important theoretical piece by Shakhnazarov which appeared twice in both complete and abbreviated versions (*Pravda* and *Mezhdunarodnaya zhizn* [*International Affairs*], the latter in English) (Shakhnazarov 1988a, 1988b).

The other principal contributors to "new thinking" (listed in Appendixes 3 and 4) include such leading party or government figures as Foreign Minister Shevardnadze and Vadim Zagladin (another of Gorbachev's personal aides), who published an important article on "global problems" as early as February 1986. V. Petrovsky, first deputy foreign minister, contributed to the elaboration of "new thinking" as early as June 1986; other contributors are heads of research institutes, such as G. Arbatov (USA and Canada Institute) and Anatolii Gromyko (Africa Institute), institute members, such as A. V. Kortunov (USA and Canada) and Y. Plimak and G. A. Trofimenko (International Workers'

*Shakhnazarov, together with Burlatsky, was instrumental in accelerating the development of sociology and political science in the Soviet Union (Shakhnazarov and Burlatsky, "O razvitii marksisto-leninskoi politicheskoi nauki" [On the development of Marxist-Leninist political science], *Voprosy filosofii* 12 [1980]; reprinted in *Soviet Law and Government* 23, 3 [Winter 1984–85]). Shakhnazarov is an expert on Western "social democracy"—a subject which has now become of special importance in Soviet relations to West European social democratic governments.

Movement), and editors of journals and newspapers or commentators, such as Alexander Bovin (*Izvestiya*), V. Afanaseev (*Pravda*), F. Burlatsky (*Literaturnaia gazeta*), I. T. Frolov (*Kommunist*), and E. Yakovlev (*Moscow News*). Many of these were already publishing during Brezhnev's time or even Khrushchev's tenure, but some can claim "maverick status" in the Soviet ideological setting.* A number of them, most notably Plimak and Kortunov, are new. They include experts on American affairs, and many have impressive backgrounds in Marxist philosophy.

All of them wrote about "new thinking" during 1986–87 in the critical period following the 27th CPSU Congress, when the concept was launched. The pattern that emerges from a comparative analysis of their articles reinforces the view of a collective effort. Individual writers seldom referred to more than a few of its aspects, and simply glossed over or made passing mention of others, in what appeared to be a mutually agreed upon understanding of the concept as a whole.†

The problem of presentation of "new thinking" was a critical aspect from the beginning because upon it would depend its domestic effect and its international impact. The launching was therefore entrusted to *Pravda*, whose editor (on a par with a Central Committee division leader) is under the direct supervision of Gorbachev and his colleagues. *Pravda* mounted a sustained campaign to promote the new concept and to instruct rank-and-file Party members and officials in its intricacies. All of Gorbachev's most important statements on the subject found their way to *Pravda*, and supplementary comments

---

*I. T. Frolov, one of Gorbachev's aides, has remarked the connection of a number of "new thinkers" to each other, noting that most of the future "Gorbachevites" served between 1958 and 1964 in Prague on the editorial board of *Problemy mira i sotsializma* under the intellectual leadership of Aleksey Rumyantsev. The group he mentions includes Frolov himself, Shakhnazarov, A. S. Chernayev, V. Zagladin (all aides to Gorbachev) as well as G. Gerasimov (Gorbachev's spokesman), Yakovlev, A. Bovin, Len Karpinskiy and others from research institutes (the think-tanks of reform) such as Oleg Bogomolov and Georgi Arbatov (P. Garimberti, "Gorbachev Aide on 'Intellectual' Leadership Style," *La Repubblica*, 16–17 April 1989; reprinted in FBIS-SOV-89-074, 19 April 1989).

†For example, Berner and Dahm (1987: 5) express disappointment that Primakov's important article entitled "New Philosophy of Foreign Policy" does not deal with philosophy.

by Politburo members were published there or in the Party weekly *Kommunist*. Important statements on "new thinking" were also published in *MEMO*, the journal put out by the Institute for International Politics and Economics (IMEMO), and since the new "world-view" implied changes in ideology and philosophy, it was discussed in a number of important articles in *Voprosy filosofii* [Questions of philosophy]. Articles on "new thinking" appeared in other journals, but irregularly, and often after their prior publication in *Pravda*. The crucial point is that "new thinking" is a Party-sponsored concept and not a product either of glasnost or of spontaneous discussions on issues other than international relations that developed in minor Soviet newspapers and journals.

It is not without significance that *Pravda* alone among the newspapers published a series of cartoons popularizing what purport to be the main ideas behind "new thinking." (See the examples in Appendix 5 below.) The same associations are repeated so often in the cartoons that it appears there may have been some official doubts about the public's ability, when confronted with such notions as "new" and "thinking," to make the right connections if left to their own devices. Certainly the ideas that the cartoonist seeks to convey—salvation of the world and escape from the nuclear impasse—are not those which, viewed against a Soviet background, would most readily come to mind. A frequently repeated theme is that of the world as a personified globe. The globe is depicted as threatened, diseased, or otherwise endangered and being saved from its predicament not by a worker, as would be expected, but by Dr. "New Thinking," who prescribes a nostrum. Or a crane-truck labelled "New Thinking" lifts the globe from a quicksand of weaponry. In combination with glasnost and perestroika (with which it is consistently conjoined), "new thinking" is the sun that melts the snowman of the cold war and dissolves the notion of Soviet threat. It is also the palette with whose rosy colors the globe can paint new idylls. Anti-Western political cartoons have always been popular in the Soviet press, and the "new thinking" series came into being in mid-1987 when the concept first began to gain momentum.

Since late 1987 "new thinking" is no longer a preoccupation only of the "inner circle," and now constitutes part of the essential vocabulary of every political scientist and journalist. Whereas early on the articles dealing with "new thinking" numbered only a couple of dozen a year, the annual count now would run into the hundreds. The number of authors also has substantially increased to include many previously unknown. *Pravda* carries a regular column on "new thinking," and the concept itself or its associated principles have become a mandatory part of any discussion of international relations. In fact the commandment to "think new" has already become a constraint on thinking and a new ideological axiom.

Helpful prompting by the Politburo would be a not unreasonable explanation of the sudden upsurge in academic debate on "new thinking."* Whatever the cause, the discussion has certainly widened—in quantitative terms—while simultaneously retaining much of its traditional Soviet homiletic character, with author after author (particularly the relatively unknown) falling into the same traps of paraphrase and plagiarism that beset the Western undergraduate and Soviet publishing of an earlier era.

Chronology of Soviet "New Thinking"

The chronologies of the development of "new thinking" by those few Western authors who acknowledge that it merits attention differ quite significantly.† Berner and Dahm (1987), for example, refer to

---

*E.g., at the All-Union Meeting of Chairmen of Departments of Social Sciences, see especially the addresses by Gorbachev and Ligachev, Dobrynin and Shevardnadze (*Pravda*, 2 October 1986). More recently, "Theses for the 19th Conference of the CPSU" spell out the areas that are in need of "scientific research."

†The Soviets' own chronology of "new thinking" dates its beginning (as do we) to the April 1985 plenum of the Central Committee—that is, one month after Gorbachev became General Secretary. Soviet writers repeatedly emphasize that "new thinking" is not only thinking but also action, and accordingly they treat Soviet diplomatic (particularly disarmament) initiatives and theoretical statements on an equal par. The actions begin with the self-imposed Soviet testing "moratorium" and the January 1986 proposal to denuclearize the world by the year 2000, and include the outcomes of Soviet-American summits (most notably the INF treaty). In the theoretical sphere, Soviet writers divide credit for the development of "new thinking" among the top party bodies—namely, the CPSU Central Committee plenum, Congress, Conference, and General Secretary Gorbachev. (The annual or semiannual meetings of the Central Committee of the CPSU are referred to by the month in which they convened—the "April plenum" in 1986, the "June plenum" in 1987, the "January plenum" and the "September plenum" in 1988—interspersed with larger and even more important CPSU

stages in the development of "new thinking" in the same way it has become customary to speak of stages in the development of perestroika. According to Berner and Dahm, the first stage coincides with the publication during 1987 of the articles dealing with the concept by Bovin, Falin, and Proektor—and particularly Primakov's "New Philosophy of Foreign Policy" (1987a). The second stage, according to Berner and Dahm, begins with Gorbachev's September 1987 article entitled "Reality and Guarantees for a Secure World" (1987b), published in all major Soviet newspapers. A third stage is heralded, according to Berner,* by an unpublished address by Shevardnadze to the 19th Conference of the CPSU in 1988. (The content has been approximated in an article by Izyumov and Kortunov entitled "The Soviet Union in the Changing World," *Mezhdunarodnaya zhizn*, July 1988; reprinted in English in *International Affairs*, August 1988.)

The progression of thought through these three stages suggests an increasing realism. Indeed each new stage seems to erode the spirit of the stage before, reducing "new thinking" to realistic pragmatism—a descent to earth from the "new thinking" heights. In our view it is misguided to look for breaks between stages, if by such breaks are meant parting company with the stage before. Perhaps "waves" would better convey the nature of the sequences of "new thinking's" development—the focus of concern of each wave differing in form, but renewing and reinforcing the one before. None of the ideas advanced in the early part of the development has been rescinded. The first wave sets the terms of reference, outlining the revised Marxist contours of "new thinking" and explaining the need

---

gatherings: the 27th CPSU Congress [February 1986] and the 19th CPSU All-Union Conference [June 1988]). Much has been made of various speeches by Gorbachev (the address on the anniversary of the Great October Revolution in October 1987, the Vladivostok speech of July 1986, the Krasnoyarsk speech of 1988, and his address to the United Nations in December 1988. Also noted are his September 1987 article entitled "Reality and Guarantees for a Secure World," Shevardnadze's address to the United Nations of September 1988, and the resolutions adopted at the 42nd and 43rd sessions of the UN General Assembly. Also listed as part of the "new thinking" literature are various documents adopted by the WTO and CMEA and, of particular importance, the "Delhi Declaration" concluded between the USSR and India in November 1986. There are no comparable listings of important articles on "new thinking" by Soviet writers.

*Based on private conversation with Berner in Miami, November 1988.

to "think new." The second wave adds the theoretical perspective of international relations—giving scope to Gorbachev's sortie into the theory of the states-system, the system of security, international organizations, and so on. The third wave does not (as we understand Berner's thinking) annul the import of the two preceding waves—to suggest there is no need or reduced need for "new thinking" or for the restructuring of the security system. Instead there is now rationalization of changed Soviet regional priorities taken against a sober financial assessment of the earlier costly involvements in the Third World. In other words, a recasting of a new Soviet foreign policy strategy takes place. The development along these lines is logical and reflected in our ordering of chapters 3–6: "new thinking" as Marxism, as theory of international relations, as international law, and as foreign policy strategy. If the presentation of "new thinking" had been in reverse order, with early revelation of the enormous cost of foreign policy involvement in the Third World preceding or in conjunction with public admissions of domestic economic problems, "new thinking" might not have come off at all.

As we have already noted, one of the distinguishing features of "new thinking" has been the intelligence behind its conception, its elaboration, and the timing of its presentation. The original team responsible for its enunciation consisted of thinkers and policymakers of high intellectual caliber who could boast an intimate knowledge of Marxism and more than a passing acquaintance with Western theories of international relations. Only with the aid of persons so qualified could Gorbachev have included in his political report words and phrases keyed to certain ideas that awaited only the requisite signal for their elaboration. The identification and full import of the key words and phrases has become clear only in retrospect as they are singled out for elaboration in bursts of Soviet writing.

Instead of being abrogated or swept aside by the succeeding waves of conceptual development, the central ideas of "new thinking" are elaborated in increasing detail and brought together to constitute in outline a renaissance of Marxism and a new Marxist theory of international relations. The liberties now being taken by Soviet commentators, and the unprecedented degree of tolerance being shown by the authorities, can only be explained by circumstances in which new ideological parameters have already been drawn. Already many articles far overstep the lines previously drawn by the censor. Only a short time ago they would have been labelled "revisionist" and qualified the writer concerned for an abrupt termination of career. The current rehabilitation of many Soviet thinkers whose thinking was terminated in the 1920s and 1930s, but who were indisputably Marxist-Leninist, would seem to bear out our interpretation of "new thinking" as a massive revision of Marxism-Leninism, without which a renaissance of Marxism in Soviet society would not be possible. By earlier standards, Soviet "new thinkers" display considerable courage because in effect they have contrived a partial refutation of Lenin despite the much emphasized filial link. By undoing a significant component part of Leninism—namely, the theory of imperialism—"new thinking" has already matched Lenin's theoretical contribution. "New thinking" will carry Soviet Marxism into a post-Leninist, post–theory of imperialism stage as soon as its elements become woven into the fabric of Marxist historical materialism. This much revision is an obligatory step for the Soviet Union to take if it wishes to use Marxism both as an intellectual tool and as the source of legitimation of its political system—one of the ideological axioms that is not negotiable.

If our analysis is correct, "new thinking" will change the Soviet Union from a totalitarian dictatorship, in which genuine thinking is proscribed, without installing in its place a Western type of intellectual pluralism with ideas developing within a context of freedom of thought and freedom of expression. Instead the USSR may change into something akin to the kind of Marxist state that would have developed in Germany or France had Marx and Engels been correct in their forecasts of proletarian revolutions in Western Europe.

We propose to explore the possibility that "new thinking" might transform the Soviet Union into something unprecedented in world history—namely, a Marxist (i.e., authoritarian) superpower that has as one of its aims the resumption of its intellectual development from the point at which it was brought to a close by Stalin. In turning back the Marxist clock to before Stalinism, the Soviet Union might find solutions to such contemporary problems as ethnic unrest. For example, the Austro-Marxist suggestion of a confederation—or genuine federation of nations and/or ethnic groups—could appeal to the new generation of Soviet "inter-ethnic" troubleshooters. Soviet "new thinkers" might succeed in the restoration of Marxist thought as an intellectual force—a transformation which, many Western Marxists assure us, it is perfectly capable of achieving.

Although such an assessment of "new thinking" would sound quite reasonable to German or even some British students of the USSR, it is not one that, to our knowledge, has so far been seriously considered in the United States. And yet it is an interpretation anticipated by the Soviets themselves (for example, in a cartoon in which glasnost, perestroika, and "new thinking" are portrayed as the new Soviet threat—see Appendix 5).

In the following two chapters, we offer some substantiation of these propositions. Both Chapters 2 and 3 deal with "new thinking" as Marxism and as theory of international relations, and the rather arbitrary line dividing them is determined primarily by a shifting emphasis on Marxism (chapter 2) or on theory of international relations (chapter 3).

In our use of sources, we take note of explicit differences between Soviet writers in the rare instances where these occur, but the authors we cite are more or less random examples of the general thrust of writings about "new thinking."

Chapter 3

"NEW THINKING" AS MARXISM OR
MARXISM-LENINISM

> "New Thinking" is a correct understanding
> of new realities subjected to analysis by the
> method of dialectical materialism.
>
> *Gorbachev*

> The 27th CPSU Congress placed the empha-
> sis on the dialectics of the unity and struggle
> of opposites in today's world . . . [correct-
> ing] the distortion under which the confron-
> tation of the two world systems . . . was
> regarded apart from their interdependence.
>
> *Primakov*

Beyond Marxism?

Although clearly written in the Marxist-Leninist idiom, articles directed at Western audiences that explicitly address "new thinking" and statements by Gorbachev do not as a rule include Marxism among the things that are "new." As a result, many commentators conclude that "new thinking" has nothing much to do with Marx-ism-Leninism, and that the superseded "old" parts include the "ir-retrievably moribund" Marxism-Leninism (Janson 1987: 5). Certainly none of the nine associated principles strikes them as conspicuously Marxist.

The confusion surrounding the compatibility of "new thinking" with Marxism is consistent with the widespread tendency to underestimate or overlook its philosophical/ideological elements. No Western commentator (as far as we are aware) has even considered the possibility that "new thinking" contains not only the nine "neutral" points, but that these can be incorporated within the

Marxist intellectual framework. Various authors argue to the contrary that the ideas that comprise "new thinking" will lead both to the end of Soviet ideology and the end of Marxism (Shenfield 1987; Howard 1987; Light 1987; R. F. Miller 1988). (These two eventualities are not regarded in the West as necessarily identical.)

The "end of Marxism" thesis revolves around the demise of the concept of class in Soviet "new thinking." Its demise is attributed to a number of factors. It has been remarked, for example, that the new concept of interdependence contradicts not only the Marxist-Leninist categories of class, class struggle, and class approach, but also conflicts with the dualist view of the world as consisting of two systems—capitalist and socialist.* The concept of interdependence is also deemed incompatible with dialectics,† and is allegedly at variance with the Soviet notion of correlation of forces which, if Gorbachev's group prevails, it threatens to replace as the centerpiece of the Soviet theory of international relations (Shenfield 1987: 7). According to Light (1987: 235), the concept of interdependence additionally means Soviet acceptance of co-responsibility for the predicaments of international politics.

The demise of the class concept in Soviet thought is also the presumed result of the introduction into "new thinking" of the *global* analytical level (of humanity, human survival, all-human values, and so forth): the Marxist notion of class struggle as the "principal motive force in international relations" is therefore allegedly at an end (R. F. Miller 1988: 16). Soviet writers do not deny the fact that the introduction of the global analytical level constitutes something of a theoretical problem. In fact the superiority of mankind's interests over class interests is often acknowledged by Soviet writers as the defining feature of "new thinking,"** and in the opinion of Gorbachev himself, the "question of combining class and universal human principles in actual world development" is "the fundamental

---

*Articles such as Bunkina and Petrov (1986) have given rise to these views with the notion of an all-world economy defined as "that economic system in which there takes place the reproduction of the total social product of the planet Earth, within which the world-socialist and world-capitalist economies interact."

†E.g., G. Jukes; quoted in S. Harris, "USSR: Gorbachev's Vladivostok Initiative," *AFAR*, March 1987, p. 113.

**See Burlatsky's reply to the question "What Is the 'New Thinking'?" in an interview with *L'Unita*, FBIS-SOV-88-212, 2 November 1988.

theoretical question that urgently confronts both Marxists and their opponents."* It is so fundamental that Ligachev's hesitation to lean toward the global, favoring instead the class aspect of the dialectical equation, contributed to his demotion. Western commentators offer their own conclusion that the global analytical level necessarily transcends the Marxist-Leninist categories of class, class approach, etc.— that it leads in the direction of a supraclass, or superclass, non-Marxist approach stripped of its commitment to world revolution, which is regarded as fundamental to Marxist theory. Other Western assumptions regarding dislodged Marxist principles include the belief that the theoretical renunciation of war in international relations is incompatible with Marxism because of its avowal of the un-Marxist concept of peace. It is argued that the disconnecting of the twin concepts of peace and socialism, which for a Marxist have always been inseparable, provides further confirmation of a rejected Marxism. To those Western commentators who argue any of these positions, the introduction of "new thinking" is subversive—not only of Soviet ideology and Marxism but of the Soviet system as a whole.

These criticisms are not easy to answer without lengthy excursions into Marxist exposition of dialectics, the class approach, socialism and capitalism, theory of imperialism, war and peace. In this chapter we argue that, rather than casting doubt on its Marxist credentials, "new thinking" can be seen to fit within the context of modern Marxism, by which we mean Marxism as one of the major contemporary philosophical traditions, with which Soviet Marxism-Leninism parted company at some point in the 1920s.† Although the concepts allegedly subversive of Marxism can be seen in mutual

---

*Gorbachev's address to the February Plenum of the CPSU, 1988.

†It was that parting of the ways that so shocked the German Marxist Karl Korsch when in 1924, at the Fifth Congress of the Comintern, his work and that of Hungarian Marxist Georg Lukacs were deemed heretical and attacked by Zinoviev and Stalin. In fact Korsch was witnessing early signs of that "paradigmatic shift," as Douglas Kellner puts it, toward "scientific Marxism" that was under way in the USSR following the death of Lenin, and that helped prepare the way for Stalinism. The attack on Korsch and Lukacs signalled the onset of the process (Kellner, "Remarks on Alvin Gouldner's 'The Two Marxisms,'" *Theory and Society* 10 [1981]: 266, 276). It remains to be seen whether Gorbachev's promises to "creatively develop" historical materialism, and the concept of dialectics in particular, will in any way change perceptions of the Marxist genealogy of the Soviet Union in the West.

contradiction *within the context of earlier dogmatic Soviet formulations,* the "case against Marxism" cannot rest there. For if Gorbachev and his team give up these earlier formulations of Marxism-Leninism, and use Marxist categories (as they frequently affirm is their intention) not as dogma but "creatively" (to use their word), then we should forget the incompatibility with Soviet Marxist-Leninist dogma and look elsewhere—specifically toward the question of the compatibility of the principles of "new thinking" with the European Marxist tradition. It is our opinion that the elements of "new thinking"that conflict with Soviet Marxism-Leninism do not stand in contradiction with the corpus of Marxist thought. We do not underestimate the intellectual obstacles that bestrew the path of any Marxist, Soviet or Western, who attempts to come to grips with world politics and economics, but the traditional argument that international relations are intractable in Marxism should not serve as an excuse for shirking the examination of "new thinking" as Marxism. We shall try to show that "new thinking" on international relations can assist in the renaissance of Marxism in the Soviet Union—a process that is being encouraged in other areas of Soviet thought. If, as is often the case in the West (cf. Brzezinski 1989), "old thinking" is equated with the Stalinist dogma that held sway over Soviet thinking for almost half a century, then, we argue, "new thinking" is a Westernized form of Marxism which, as with Western Marxism generally, is becoming increasingly "Hegelianized." In Soviet writings to date, the "Hegelianization" of Soviet Marxism can be found both in a new emphasis placed on the concept of dialectics and in a relaxed form of historical materialism that goes beyond the Bukharin/Lenin theory of imperialism.

Without some understanding of the meaning (both past and present) of such concepts as dialectics, it is difficult to appreciate the direction of development of Soviet "new thinking," as well as some of the important statements made with reference to it. The exploration of the path(s) taken by *Western* Marxists in their recently augmented efforts to conceptualize international relations are particularly germane in this context, for they provide insights into both what Marxism can offer and what Marxism-Leninism has failed to offer. The study of Western Marxism, in other words, enables us to foresee what Gorbachev's "new thinkers" are likely to produce by way of Marxist explanations of international politics.

As we follow these often meandering Marxist paths, we shall pause at appropriate junctures to highlight the concepts that are allegedly under threat from "new thinking," but that in many cases appear to us to involve a strengthening of Marxism.

Marxism and International Relations: The Range of the Possible

Marx, as we know, left his heirs rather unprepared for handling international politics.* Not only did he misconceive the future course of development of capitalism and the states-system, but he grossly underestimated the staying power of both—in particular, that of the states-system, whose prolonged coexistence with the capitalist mode of production he considered a theoretical impossibility. In his optimistic faith in stateless world communism, he left a sizable gap in his theory with no blueprint for anyone seeking to apply Marxism to international relations.

It is a gap which Marxists are now required to bridge. It separates, on the one hand, Marx's analysis of capitalism within states (with its expectations of simultaneous revolutions inside states) and, on the other hand, the stateless future society of world communism. The usable legacy is mainly a methodology, which, in many of Marx's heirs, involves an obsessive search for classes. Despite its universalism, Marxist tradition has tended to define itself on the domestic level in terms of major conflicts between classes. International or global concepts and values, as well as concepts derivative from the states-system, with which Marxists must now come to terms, such as peace, national self-determination, decolonization, global equality, sovereignty, anti-nuclearism, and so forth, do not fit comfortably into classical Marxism, and their opposites could as easily be substituted.

As Lenin and other early Soviet theorists of international law and international relations were to see, international politics has been something of a nightmare for all Marxists—namely, how to explain the superstructure and substructure of the whole planet? It was an almost intractable problem for the Soviet theorists of the 1920s and

*For a detailed discussion, see Kubálková and Cruickshank (1985, 1989: chs. 1 and 10).

early 1930s who were still allowed to "think creatively"—before the Stalinist purges put an end to axiom-free Marxist thinking in the Soviet Union. The early Soviet theorists such as E. B. Pashukanis and E. A. Korovin anticipated many of the issues of the 1980s when they sought to explain why, if the substructure of the world was broken up into socialist and capitalist states, all shared the same norms of international law as a part of a global superstructure.*

The question of the theoretical relation of the capitalist mode of production to the states-system was especially difficult: how to relate a form of production driven by the pursuit of individual profit with the pursuit of the national interests of states. Following heated discussions at the time of the Second International, it was the Bukharin/Lenin theory of imperialism that prevailed and became the foundation for Soviet thinking on international relations (as well as for many Western Marxists in the recent upsurge in popularity of theories of dependency, neo-imperialism, and World-System).

According to the Bukharin/Lenin theory of imperialism, the fates of capitalism and of the states-system had become inextricably intertwined. The capitalist mode of production, according to Bukharin, adjusted itself to the states-system and thereby extended its life span. Capitalists in their pursuit of profits could begin availing themselves of an array of states-system mechanisms, especially imperialist expansionist wars.† Thus conflict in international relations, and the states-system itself, could be explained in terms of the dynamics of capitalism. Capitalism and war were necessarily conjoined, and conversely socialism became synonymous with peace.

Thus concepts of international relations have always occupied a secondary place in Marxist theory—their importance dependent on their relationship to the major class struggles of a given period. Marxist theories of international relations could make some sense only if a class explanation could be found for interstate relations. As a result, the level of abstraction that characterizes the discipline of international relations, which emerged in the United Kingdom and the United States a year or so after the USSR came into existence, can never be accepted by Marxists—and particularly not by Western Marxists. To Soviet Marxist-Leninists, the states-system can never be

*For a summary of these issues see, for example, Kubálková and Cruickshank (1985, 1989: ch. 8).

†N. Bukharin, *Imperialism and World Economy* (New York: H. Wertig, 1966).

homogeneous so long as there are a variety of socioeconomic modes of production. Marxists see capitalist and socialist states as arbitrarily lumped together in a generic category—states—much too abstract for their policies to be judged by the same yardstick. In Soviet Marxism-Leninism, the concept of socialism and capitalism as socioeconomic "systems" was, as Shakhnazarov argues, virtually replaced by the concept of "states belonging to different social and economic formations." As a consequence the idea of competition between socialism and capitalism—in Soviet Marxism-Leninism the modern derivative of the concept of class struggle—took on the characteristics of interstate relations (Shakhnazarov 1988a: 17), giving relations between capitalist and socialist blocs of states a fiercely conflictual (even "threatening") aspect. Given the perception of the world as based on a "global class struggle" between socialism and capitalism, the states-system has always been seen as in an unstable condition not conducive to cooperative involvement by the USSR—an attitude particularly evident in formulating the concepts of "socialism in one country" and "capitalist encirclement."

The crucial question of the relation between the states-system and modes of production has become one of the most difficult to resolve. A number of alternative solutions have been put forward by Western Marxists, who unlike Soviet Marxist-Leninists are spared the necessity of coming up with a theoretical foundation for foreign policy decisions. One of these alternatives is to ignore the states-system altogether. This is a solution that many Western academic Marxists find acceptable because it would allow the continued development of Marxism as a theory of *domestic* society. Another possibility put forward is that of relaxing the strictures of historical materialism and granting the autonomy of the states-system. Another proposal, made by the Austro-Marxist Hilferding, goes even further: it would separate the states-system from modes of production altogether and treat them as entities apart, with the dynamic of one not reducible to that of the other. We see below that in this regard it is Hilferding's position, generally overlooked by Marxists until now, that has found its way into Soviet "new thinking."

At all events theoretical difficulties abound—not only in stretching Marxist categories to the level of states but in extending them to the global analytical level prior to the achievement of world communism.

Dialectics

Marxism as a mode of thought can more than compensate for its apparent difficulties with the concept of international relations. Its internal features allow for enormous flexibility, which facilitates its survival as a mode of thought. Like history (as Raymond Aron puts it), Marxism is inexhaustible and ambiguous. It cannot be surpassed because it contains the method of its own transcendence (Lefebvre).

This capability is due largely to one of its principal concepts—dialectics. It is the concept that Lenin designated as the very "spirit" of Marxist teaching and that Gorbachev has stressed time and again is the key to the "creative" development of Marxism that is now to take place in the Soviet Union. For this reason alone, some comment on its meaning is essential—not in its dogmatic Soviet usage, nor as the caricature it became in Stalinism, but in terms of its potential insofar as that can be ascertained from its usage in Western Marxism.

There can be little doubt that dialectics was the most neglected part of Marxism in Soviet Marxism-Leninism. In Soviet textbooks it is illustrated by referring to Engels's fatuous imagery of butterflies cavorting in the butterfly mating season. The mating of the first butterfly ("thesis") with the second ("antithesis") gives rise to the qualitatively different "synthesis" of thousands upon thousands of butterflies. As befits Engels's imagery, dialectics and its laws came to mean nothing at all. To say two things are dialectically related amounts in the Soviet usage to a tautological restatement of the same problem, without shedding any light on the relationship. One might as well say that any two things or processes are related dialectically so long as they are not identical.

Dialectics does not have to be fatuous, however. It has a quite respectable, if limited, place in Western philosophy; its progenitors include not only Marx and Engels, but also Aristotle and Hegel. American Marxist Bertell Ollman uses it as the key concept of his Marxism, and Hayward Alker defines his non-Marxist approach to international relations—the "radical dialectical" paradigm—as one of only three possible approaches to the study of international relations.*

*Alker and Biersteker (1984).

Intellectually the concept of dialectics has much to offer. As we noted years before it entered Soviet ideology through "new thinking,"* the concept of interdependence, once fashionable in Western studies of international relations, *inheres* in the dialectical approach, which in essence sees things as interconnected and interdependent. To say that two things are related dialectically does not there-have to be tautologous. The choice of a dialectical method indicates a rejection of the monocausal approach and the notion of unilinear development in favor of the dynamic, multicausal and multidirectio-nal. Dialectics sees things as inevitably interconnected and inter-dependent. Preoccupied with conflict and contradiction, those applying the dialectical method seek to understand change in terms of study of the past and present while establishing a connection between future developments and the present. Dialecticians never see cause and effect in an isolated, unilinear development, but per-ceive reciprocal causalities where everything both influences and is influenced by others individually and holistically.

Dialectics can be used as an *ontological* theory dealing with the material world and/or history, or it can be used as an *epistemological* theory concerning the nature of knowledge of the material world. Dialectical reasoning lends itself to presentation in models and so-phisticated mathematical formulas.

Materialist dialectics or Lenin's "dialectical materialism" adopts dialectics for both its ontological thesis and its epistemological thesis. Because it is a materialist dialectics, it sees the dialectical inter-dependencies (that is to say, the reciprocal causalities) as asymmetri-cal, with the more material aspects being regarded as weightier, more influential, indeed prior. As an epistemological theory, dialectical ma-terialism conceives of man as "real, active man." The constructive nature of human consciousness, it is argued, cannot be reduced to mere cognition. For Marx, cognitive action is material and practical, and so knowledge is not merely a cognitive reflection upon an external world, but becomes—to use the formulation of a Western Marxist theorist of international relations—the means for shaping and there-fore changing reality.† This notion has been encapsulated in the Soviet

*V. Kubálková and A. A. Cruickshank, *International Inequality* (London: Croom Helm, 1981), p. 56.

†John Maclean, "Marxist Epistemology, Explanation of 'Change' and the Study of International Relations," in *Change and the Study of International Relations*, eds. Barry Buzan et al. (London: Frances Pinter, 1981), p. 55.

maxim of the unity of theory and practice, with its characteristic subordination, until now, of theory to practice—a maxim rejected by most Western philosophical systems.

Historical Materialism

Historical materialism (so labelled by Plekhanov) is the extension of dialectical materialism to history and society. In the recent revival among Western Marxists of historical materialism as a method, it has come to mean different things to different people. Minimally historical materialism refers to the asymmetries found in history and society—the reciprocal causal relation within such paired Marxist categories as superstructure-substructure, relations of production-forces of production, and consciousness-being—where it is always the side more directly related to matter (hence materialist) which is the weightier of the two and ultimately determines the less weighty of the paired categories. Thus historical materialist studies of history and society are based on asymmetrical types of interdependence in which economic factors (related to modes of production and/or classes) are emphasized.

In the joining of materialism with dialectics, there are two contradictory influences on Marx (i.e., Feuerbach and Hegel), and preference for one or the other of these influences divides Marxists into "Hegelians" (emphasizing dialectics) and "anti-Hegelians" (emphasizing materialism). The Hegelians are further divided into "antinomists " and "polarists." To a polarist, contradiction means simply a material difference between two polar aspects of one entity leading to a collision. Polarism is implicit in the Soviet idea of two sharply separated, mutually isolated world socioeconomic systems. To the antinomist, contradiction goes beyond collision to mutual interpenetration: capitalism contains elements of non-capitalism and socialism of non-socialism.* As Alker has shown in his theory of international

---

*This position is best summarized by the new chairman of the Ideological Commission, Medvedev: "The idea that socialism and capitalism can develop somehow in parallel is . . . obsolete. On the contrary, the paths of their development inevitably cross, and both systems inevitably interact within the framework of one and the same human civilization. Of course, there can be no talk about any convergence of the two systems, nor of their fusion. Each one continues to develop according to its own laws" (*Pravda*, 5 October 1988).

relations, the effect of one party to a contradiction interpenetrating the other is to blur the original distinguishing features of both. In the present case, it is a formula asking for application to the Soviet aspiration to "integrate in all possible ways" with the capitalist international economy/technology, etc., where the reciprocal spread of elements of socialism, such as trade unionism, social welfare, and the like, in capitalism can also be assumed.

The process we feel is fostered by Soviet "new thinking" is the tendency, apparent throughout the twentieth century, to neutralize the characteristics of asymmetry—what is often referred to as the Hegelianization of historical materialism. Stalin gave in to this tendency for practical reasons, rather than on philosophical grounds. As seen by contemporary Western historical materialists, it appears that economic-related forces—the weightier of the paired categories—are merely limiting the range of possible variations of development. Most Marxists in the twentieth century have managed to weaken economic determinism, and with it reduced the importance of the concepts of class and class struggle, and have attempted to reverse the asymmetry of historical development in favor of granting greater "autonomy" to the political superstructure. As Norberto Bobbio puts it, referring to Gramsci: "A Marxist . . . remains a Marxist so long as he simply accepts a dichotomy between superstructure and substructure, analytically holds them apart, and/or recognizes that the economy *always* is determinant 'in the last instance'"—no matter how distant that "instance" might be.* Thus, in the tradition of Lukacs and Gramsci, it is permissible for a historical materialist to assert the primacy of ideological superstructure over the economic substructure, which in Gramsci's case becomes the primacy of civil society (based on consensus) over political society (based on force). A caricature of this theme was the Stalinist notion of "revolution from above"—a concept which Gorbachev still uses.

A historical sociology of international relations that historical materialist methodology produces presents a picture of a world very different from that of the international relations realist mainstream, and different also from the earlier Stalinist formulations. To paraphrase the Western Marxist Robert Cox, it is a picture based on complex patterns of interacting social forces in which states play an

*In C. Mouffe, ed., *Gramsci and Marxist Theory* (London: Routledge and Kegan Paul, 1979), p. 3.

intermediate, even autonomous, role between global and social structures, together with ideas and ideologies.* Similarly, a Soviet writer observes that the formation of socialism and its supersession of the capitalist system is an all-embracing historical process that is manifested in more than the development of socialist countries (Shakhnazarov 1988a: 17).

Instead of simply gauging the "balance of power" among states, Marxists have to try to comprehend the "state of the world" by use of a more broadly encompassing conceptual prism. This "prism," referred to by Lenin as the "current moment," becomes Althusser's "conjuncture," subsequently Cox's "historical structure" or "historical conjuncture," and the Soviet "correlation of forces." In Althusser's words, it refers to "the central concept of the science of politics . . . denoting the exact balance of force concept at any given moment to which political tactics must be applied." This includes not only the strength of states, but also various other class formations (domestic and international), ideas, ideologies, and institutions as these enter the equation.† The Soviet concept of "correlation of forces," in the context of its Marxist lineage, is a gauge for assessing the current moment in world history. In comparison with the Western gauge of "balance of power," its finely tuned calibrations are sensitive to actors other than states and to a much wider range of factors than simply military strength ratios.

The current reading of the correlation of forces, according to Gorbachev and his colleagues, indicates the interdependence of states and nations, of capitalism and socialism. In the Soviet sense, therefore, correlation of forces and interdependence can hardly be in contradiction—their relation is akin to that of a seismograph and an earthquake. Continuing with the same simile, if dialectics deals with the earth's plates (the motion of matter and thought), it can hardly be superseded by the concept of interdependence, which describes a special position of the earth's plates at a particular time.

---

*"Gramsci, Hegemony and International Relations: An Essay in Method," *Millennium: Journal of International Studies* 12, 2 (1983); see also Cox, *Production, Power, and World Order: Social Forces in the Making of History* (New York: Columbia University Press, 1987).

†L. Althusser, *For Marx* (New York: Pantheon, 1969), p. 250.

Interdependence

The Soviets could not have found a Western concept more suitable to effect entry into Western political discourse than interdependence. It is a term that has gained wide popularity in the West and exercises a rare appeal, despite its lack of precise meaning. The Soviet usage of so familiar a concept, in the midst of hitherto relentless Marxist-Leninist parlance, carries a message in itself. Perhaps most impressive is the economy of effort with which intellectual connections are established. The skillful establishment in so short a time of such connections, after decades of opposition, is a remarkable achievement—enthusiastically welcomed by a highly receptive Western audience. Terms such as *interdependence*, *global*, and *all-human*, common in Western political discourse, now punctuate almost any discussion of "new thinking" that comes out of the USSR.

It is interesting to note the similarity of circumstances under which interdependence has become popular in the West and now in Soviet "new thinking." It became popular in the United States in response to the setbacks of the late 1960s and early 1970s—the stalemate in Vietnam, a troubled U.S. dollar, the adversarial conceptualization of North-South dependency, and other emerging problems of the time.* In a comparably difficult situation, the Soviets have now put the same concept at the heart of Marxism-Leninism. Beyond the circumstances in which it is adopted, however, the Soviet meaning of the concept begins to diverge.

As Jones and Willetts point out, the term *interdependence* in its American usage highlights the basic mutuality of interests among all groups of societies within the contemporary world system. But the usefulness is doubtful of a concept so broad as to comprehend such diverse views as those of the "liberal reformists" of the Brandt Commission† and proponents of "Reaganomics," who believe that maximum benefits are to be derived from an unfettered, global *laissez-faire* system. The spread of views of advocates of interdependence in the

---

*"Introduction" in R. J. Barry Jones and P. Willetts, eds., *Interdependence on Trial: Studies in the Theory and Reality of Contemporary Interdependence* (London: Frances Pinter, 1984), pp. 1–3.

†See the Brandt Commission Report of the Independent Commission on International Development Issues. I: *North-South: A Programme for Survival* and II: *Common Crisis* (London: Pan, and Cambridge, Mass.: MIT Press, 1980, 1983).

South has been equally wide, ranging from proponents of advancing the time frame for implementing the New International Economic Order (NIEO) to defenders of the interests of a Third World elite who seek the continuation of an entrenched economic system. Interestingly, the concept of interdependence is resisted only at the extremes of the ideological-political spectrum: power realists reject it as mythical* and Western Marxists as an "ideological intervention" that prevents the development of a genuinely Marxist approach to international politics.[†] Apart from these rare exceptions, however, the concept has met with unusually wide acceptance. Nevertheless, in light of its history, it would be prudent to have some reservations, and when confronted with the term to have a fairly precise knowledge of the context from which it derives. Besides details of meaning and etymology, conclusions should be based on knowledge of motivating ideologies or special interests** that always seem to lie in the background of the term of interdependence in its Western or Southern usage—or in its present employment by Soviet "new thinkers."

Historical Materialism and Interdependence

There is no doubt that, in the Soviet context, thinking about the world as interdependent has a distinctively Marxist flavor. Its roots can be traced in several directions, coming not only from the Marxist concept of dialectics, which as we have remarked postulates a sort of general system of interdependencies. Soviet writers cite Lenin's well-known dictum that the Bolsheviks "live not only in a state but in a system of states" as evidence of his awareness of interdependence—an awareness that the survival of the nascent Soviet state in its early years, as an autarky and in isolation from the rest of the (capitalist) world, depended on a rudimentary condition of interdependence. Again referring to Lenin for support of their arguments, Soviet "new thinkers" remind us that Marxism postulates an inevitable tendency of social development toward increasing "socialization" of relations of production and other associated principles. The

---

*K. Waltz, *Theory of International Politics* (Reading, Mass.: Addison-Wesley, 1979).

[†]J. Maclean, in Jones and Willetts.

**Jones and Willetts.

end result of that tendency is their "globalization," of which a global economy is only the beginning.

Finally, and most important in regard to Soviet usage of interdependence, there is a long tradition in Marxist thought of the idea of a military threat to humanity's survival that harks back to Rosa Luxemburg's "catastrophism"*—which is anticipated in Engels's fear that humanity is developing a destructive potential that threatens its existence.† There was an early warning in Luxemburg's famous dictum "socialism or barbarism": that unless socialism prevails, humanity will perish as a result of the inherent tendency of the capitalist mode of production to self-destruct. For the first time in decades, Luxemburg is cited by and receives the approbation of Soviet writers.**

Since the current understanding of interdependence in the USSR is derived from all these sources, it overlaps only partially with Western interpretations. The Soviet concept lacks the complexity and sophistication of the vast Western literature on the subject. Soviet "new thinking" endorses the liberal reformist description of the symptoms of interdependence, but orders them differently along lines of their perceived importance. Where, as Marxists, the Soviet "new thinkers" would be expected to be oriented primarily toward the concept of economic interdependence as a progression of the historical materialist idea of the globalization of social development, the Soviet concept is instead explained primarily by reference to the "global problems of mankind," with emphasis on those of the "catastrophist" variety. Unlike the majority of their Western counterparts, they see the global economy of interdependence as of less immediate concern, to be dealt with at some future time. The reason is obvious: the economic interdependence between socialist and capitalist countries is not yet at a level to justify discussion of the mutual "sensitivities" or "vulnerabilities" of the participants in interdependent relationships. In fact most Western writing that deals with relations of economic interdependence in the world ignores both the USSR and the socialist system. This is a situation that Soviet economic

*The Accumulation of Capital (London: Routledge, 1951).

†See W. B. Gallie, Philosophers of Peace and War: Kant, Clausewitz, Marx, Engels, and Tolstoy (Cambridge: Cambridge University Press, 1978).

**V. Zagladin, Peace and Disarmament (Moscow, 1982), pp. 39–40.

policymakers will try to remedy, and with the generous support of Western financiers (already primed for over a decade to think in terms of the inevitability of economic interdependence), they will surely succeed.

The idea of interdependence that is embodied in "new thinking" is, in other words, a very special, *sui generis* subtype of the Western concept. It is based on a perception of exposure to a common threat. Zagladin (1986a: 9) recognizes two "dialectically related" sources of interdependence-producing global problems: a "universally human" and a "social." He acknowledges that the former has traditionally been neglected by Soviet analysts, but that is no longer the case, and the discussion of all-human global problems has become a mandatory part of the discussion of "new thinking." The list of global problems is headed by those that stem from the nuclear threat,* and they receive commensurate attention: "Over the all-human home of ours hangs the nuclear threat," warns Gorbachev (1986a: 12); "no one can be saved" on the endangered "cosmic ship Earth," says Petrovsky (1986: 6, 3); it is an "interdependence of fate," observes Morozov (1986: 6); and Plimak has fears concerning "survival" and "self-preservation" (1987: 1)

Soviet commentators believe that nuclear and other global problems unite humanity, or at least prompt people to come together in cooperative arrangements. At this point, however, they depart from liberal reformist discussions of interdependence. The Soviet concept of interdependence rests on the idea of globalism and a mutuality of interests that results from common exposure to the threat: it is, however, capitalism, capitalist states, that have created these problems. Global problems, indeed the "crisis of human civilisation" (Plimak 1987: 73), derive from capitalism. This view of interdependence has been expressed not only by Gorbachev, but also by other influential "new thinkers" such as Yakovlev (1986), Mshvenieradze (1986: 52), and Dobrynin (1986a: 23). There is no suggestion of Soviet acceptance of co-responsibility for the global crisis, but capitalism alone is incapable of resolving it.

This view of Soviet "new thinkers" converges with Rosa Luxemburg's "socialism or barbarism": global problems are resolvable only by a collectivist socialist system and through its methods—on the basis of "a collectivist, socialist approach" (Shakhnazarov 1988b: 17).

*For sample lists of global problems, see Zagladin (1986), Kortunov (1986), Krasin (1986), Primakov (1986), Dobrynin (1986a), and Yakovlev (1986).

Marxist Universalism

There is thus another way of looking at the global analytical level rather than seeing it as necessarily un-Marxist. It can be argued that the "new thinkers," in addressing global human problems and values, not only do not contradict Marxism, but may be said to confirm its universalism and revolutionary drive. Proponents of "new thinking" claim that it is revolutionary (Yakovlev 1986: 3), but when they say that, is it just another Marxist-Leninist cliché? We argue that there is a Marxist substance to such claims. To undertake to speak for humanity as a whole can be seen as a Soviet attempt to make the most of current circumstances by translating global problems into Marxist propositions, thereby rescuing Marxism and their credentials as Marxists at one and the same time. The emergence of global problems which has led to the discovery of humanity's interdependence has brought about a reinvigoration of the Soviets' missionary zeal. Gorbachev and others cite Lenin in support of the idea that social development is more important than that of any particular class—even the proletariat.* Whether or not, as some Sovietologists claim, this is a quotation taken out of context to legitimize "new thinking" does not matter: the classical Marxist message is unmistakably humanist, universalist, and messianic—fertile ground for the discussion of global problems.

Marx, after all, spoke on behalf of all members of society as increasingly he conceived of their joining the ranks of the proletariat. If one is cynical about the failure of the Soviet Union to preside over a global revolutionary movement, the new emphasis on interdependence and global all-human problems could be construed as an attempt to regroup. The circumstances of interdependence brought on by global problems can be seen as extending rather than abandoning the concept of class. The global problems come as something of a *deus ex machina* for a stale and spent Marxist-Leninist doctrine. Although threatening catastrophe, global problems play a positive role

*Gorbachev quotes a statement by Lenin (written in 1899, published in 1924) about the necessity of the struggle against the tsar for political freedom "not only in the interests of the working class but also in the interests of social development as a whole . . . for, from the point of view of the basic idea of Marxism, the interests of social development are higher than the interests of the proletariat" (*Sochinenia:* Polnoe Sobranie, t. 4, p. 220).

in the context of historical materialism: they produce global consciousness, out of which there emerges an "objective long-term common interest in human survival" and an "end to the alienation of
politics from the norms of morality common to all mankind"
(Gorbachev 1987e). As Gorbachev and his team see it, through the
impact of nuclear technology, humanity—not just a particular social
class—is united by the shared realization that it has lost its immortality as a species, and that all-human values—essentially peace—are
the sole guarantors of its survival.

The subordination of all other values to peace ("the highest of
them all," as Ligachev puts it in one of the earliest discussions of
this topic*) does not contradict Marxism or, for that matter, Soviet
ethics.[†] While Soviet concepts of morality and the eschatology of
values have always been ethically relativist, it has always been assumed in the Soviet theory of ethics that all moralities contain elements of "all-human morality" or "common moments of morality of
different human collectivities or classes" [sic] representative of "minimal conditions of moral life."** These invariably include the commandment "Do not kill."[††] The fully developed all-human, universally valid morality is not expected to emerge until the arrival of
communist society, but the "Thou shalt not kill" biblical imperative—
the "higher morality to ensure survival" (Petrovsky 1986: 5)—has
now been extended to the species as a whole.

This means simply that the Soviets are prepared to add a *negative*
concept of peace—namely, the absence of war—to their *positive* definition of peace as a synonym of socialism. Negatively defined peace
has never before been regarded as an absolute goal because both
war and peace were seen as extensions of politics by other means

---

*"Peace has become the highest value of humanity, more than that, a necessary
condition of its survival on the planet" (*Pravda*, 7 November 1986).

[†]One of the earliest pre-"new thinking" publications dealing with the concept
of peace as "an all-human heritage, an *absolute value*, in contradistinction to
relative values which are of significance to particular states, nations and social
groupings" is *The Planning of World Peace*, by F. Burlatsky, published in 1971 by
UNESCO, but not published in the USSR in Brezhnev's time.

**Shishkin; quoted in V. Kubálková, "Moral Precepts of Soviet Foreign Policy,"
in *Moral Claims in World Affairs*, ed. R. Pettman (London: Croom Helm, 1979),
p. 176.

[††]For confirmations of this point, see Shakhnazarov (1984).

(an endorsement of Clausewitz by both Lenin and earlier Marxists), which meant that wars might be adjudged just or unjust, depending upon who waged them and for what reasons. In Marxist-Leninist theory, peace in the positive sense as synonymous with communism or socialism is seen as a proper historical and moral aim, but the path leading to that end now has to be reassessed in the changed world of nuclear weaponry. In these circumstances, Marx's midwife of history—violence—could become its gravedigger, a point upon which Soviet writers frequently dwell (Plimak 1986; Plimak 1987: 76).

Class perspectives (believed by commentators to have been transcended) have now made a dramatic reappearance in Soviet writing. Although peace is the chief human value, other considerations remain unaltered.* Indeed class considerations enter the equation when we read that the Soviet Union is the only force (Gorbachev's "pioneer") capable of speaking on behalf of humanity as a whole, and is even prepared to compromise its foreign policy to save humanity from otherwise inevitable catastrophe. As Arbatov puts it: "New Thinking reflects the class interests of the USSR but also the basic needs of humanity" (1987: 115). Even though its sources include the works of non-Marxist writers beyond the Soviet frontiers, only the Soviet Union is capable of developing "new thinking." Of this Soviet interpretation of "new thinking" there can be no doubt; writer after writer stresses the coincidence of interests of the proletariat, humanity, and socialism in the resolution of global problems. Dobrynin observes that the "international historical mission of the working class . . . [is] . . . imbued with a new and deeper meaning for they are to save mankind" (1986a: 24).

Moreover, the coincidence of interests of the working class and mankind offers new revolutionary possibilities: the struggle for the resolution of global problems "is a part of revolution" (Shakhnazarov 1988a). The Soviet Union's friends and alliances, the "revolutionary" or "progressive" forces, are now—as befits the "new stage in

---

*Ligachev observes that "This does not mean that other realities recede into the background" (*Pravda*, 7 November 1986), while Afanaseev explains that "By giving priority to all-human values, . . . the party, class approach is not given up" (*Pravda*, 5 December 1986). See also Zhdanov, "The Proletariat Becomes Revolutionary when It Identifies with All-Human Problems" (*Pravda*, 6 March 1987).

humanity's development"—defined differently. They are joined together with humanity as a whole. The shibboleth for entry into this Soviet alliance has ceased to be articulated in economic and class symbols, but is now expressed in the patterns and phraseology of "new thinking." The global masses on behalf of whom the USSR now claims to speak are defined by their political consciousness and include the broad range of liberal, radical, social democratic, and peace movement thinkers.* Under Soviet guidance, this amalgam that the "new thinking" embraces will coalesce and develop—another part of the previously noted Hegelianization of Soviet Marxism-Leninism. The eclectic nature of "new thinking" is highlighted in calls to "further develop and enrich" Marxism-Leninism by combining it with "the humanistic and general democratic ideals of all social forces seriously concerned for the self-preservation of humanity" (Dobrynin 1986a). "New thinking" invites communists, social democrats, liberals, religious leaders, and even moderate conservatives to unite against the world nuclear threat; more often than not such a broad united front is dominated by anti-Western or anti-American sentiments.

To recapitulate: neither the concept of interdependence nor the new concept of peace and concern for humanity as a whole represent a contradiction of Marxism or a surrender of the class approach. "New thinking" is still consistent with the Marxist vision of the world. The changes introduced by the "new thinkers" are fully consistent with Marxist universalism, Marxist dialectics, and Marxist historical materialism. Soviet "new thinking" is not only a form of Marxism, but also a full-fledged Marxist theory of international relations, as we shall now proceed to argue.

---

*"The dividing line in this struggle does not usually run between classes and parties but within them" (Tomashevsky and Lukov 1985: 17).

Chapter 4

"NEW THINKING" AS A THEORY OF
INTERNATIONAL RELATIONS

Having posited "new thinking" as leading toward a possible renaissance of Marxist thinking in the Soviet Union, we see in it also the genesis of a new, very different Soviet theory of international relations. It is here that we come across the true antonym of "new thinking." Whatever its acquired or secondary meaning, "new thinking" on international relations has clearly been contrived as a critique and repudiation of the "old" Western thinking on international relations and, in particular, of Western power realism.

To explain the innovative elements of "new thinking" as a theory of international relations, we refer briefly to some of the parameters within which Western debates on international relations have taken place, and to those aspects that are relevant to an understanding of Soviet "new thinking"—in other words, the major philosophical traditions of the study of international relations and the degree of continuum of integration of states* that provide our basic terms of reference.

The conceptual continuum of the progressively increasing integration of states begins at one extreme with the simple unconnected coexistence of states. To find historical examples of that situation is much more difficult than finding examples of the next stage on the continuum—namely, *states-system* or *international system*. Within a states-system the actions of each state or group of states loom as important factors in the calculations of the others within a context of overall international anarchy and absence of globally shared values. This is the stage that power realism (the Hobbesian philosophical tradition), which is the dominant approach to international relations in the West and a foundation of U.S. strategic doctrine, sees as

*Cf. H. Bull, *The Anarchical Society* (London: Macmillan, 1977).

descriptive of the world as it is. In the view of many power realists, the states-system is a form of political organization beyond which sovereign states, fragmented by their particular interests and values, cannot in the foreseeable future be expected to proceed.

The next stage on the continuum is a closer integration of states into an international society, in which there are some shared interests and values reflected in common institutions. In the Grotian philosophical tradition, its advocates favor strengthening the core of shared interests and values through international law, international organizations, and other cooperative measures, based on the belief that there are in fact some commonly held global imperatives of morality and law.

Karl Deutsch's concept of a "pluralistic security community," evolved in the 1950s, is one of the main contemporary expressions of the Grotian tradition.* Deutsch's concept repudiates the main assumptions of power realism and the inevitability of an anarchical states-system and asserts instead a strong trend toward international collaboration via transnational processes within an increasing interdependence of states. Abandoning what he claims is the "ungovernable"† realist conception of a balance of power to deter aggression, Deutsch postulates a world of "pluralistic security communities." By no means expecting political integration into one "world state" (regarding such an outcome as neither effective nor easily maintained), he argues that a world of coexisting, increasingly more cooperative interdependent units would render obsolete the traditional system of balance of power and might make global peace attainable.

Deutsch's vision has won praise even from the international relations "left," who welcome it as providing a common denominator of a "communitarian" tradition that, in the words of one of its proponents, defines a stable social system achieved through a consensus of symbols, norms, and rights which serve to "coordinate expectations and to orient and limit practices."** According to Richard Ashley,

---

*H. Bull, "The Grotian Conception of International Society," in *Diplomatic Investigations: Essays in the Theory of International Policies*, eds. H. Butterfield and Martin Wight (London: Allen and Unwin, 1966).

†Karl W. Deutsch and J. David Singer, "Multipolar Power Systems and International Stability," *World Politics* 16, 3 (April 1964): 390–406.

**R. K. Ashley, "The Eye of Power: The Politics of World Modeling," *International Organization* 37, 3 (Summer 1983): 536.

communitarianism, derived from Deutsch's security community concept, places stress on the communicative basis of social order and posits a reality achieved through "multiple, mutually interpenetrating vantage points,"* thereby denying the supremacy of a single power authority but radically transcending the present political division into sovereign states.†

Thus critics of the Hobbesian, power realist tradition and of the states-system extant in today's world look hopefully beyond the states-system to the rationalist cooperative international society or even to a *world society* or *world community*, at the other extreme. World society refers to an integrated worldwide human society possessed of a sense of commonly held interests and values, with common rules and institutions, whether detached from the perspective of states or still retaining the states-system in its makeup.

The problem is how to effect a transition from the states-system to an international society or to a world society. Deutsch saw a possibility of progressive integration of security communities by strengthening their common political ideology and what he called "depolitization" of their relations. Hedley Bull toyed with the notion of the evolution of a world society through an initiative of the Western world, with the basis of such an arrangement in shared culture and values of "modernity." The normative theories that stress the need to advance to a world society have usually been labelled utopian or idealist, in contrast to the realist theories that have been the foundation of the (particularly American) international relations mainstream.

*Ibid., p. 534.

†Deutsch's concept is based on a study of the integration of the North Atlantic region in which, in his view, "war had been eliminated for all practical purposes," and could be regarded as "fratricidal." Among the "essential" requirements for the evolution of pluralistic security communities, Deutsch stresses a shared, or similar, political ideology and "compatibility of the main values" (in Deutsch et al., *Political Community and the North Atlantic Area: International Organization in the Light of Historical Experience* [Princeton, 1957] p. 4). A commitment to a particular economic philosophy is less essential. The *sine qua non* for Deutsch's integration is the "gradual depolitization of the region": he notes that the values of one country become dangerous to community cohesion if linked to the control of military force when "expansionism, ideological crusading, or militarism were built into the value system so firmly that they would have an important effect upon national power" (126). Other factors that Deutsch regards as prerequisites of security communities are "mutual predictability of behavior" and an attitude of confidence and trust.

Soviet and Western Theoretical Concepts

Where in this continuum does Soviet thinking—old or new—fit? It is a question that international relations theorists have seldom addressed, or have balked at the answers.

With its traditional Manichean vision of good and evil, and the class struggle between capitalist and socialist systems, Soviet theory (or for that matter, any Marxist theory) would not find a place in either the Grotian or the Hobbesian tradition. Instead it would feel kinship with what to theorists of international relations is the Kantian tradition. In the Kantian or universalist tradition, the dominant theme, though it appears to be the relationships among states, is really the relationships among all men in the human community. This relationship, even if not manifest, is conceived to exist in potential, and when it materializes will sweep the system of states into limbo. Within the community of mankind, the interests of all men are identical, with conflicts of interest existing only on a superficial or transient level among dominant groupings of states, in the conflicts of ideology that cut across state boundaries and divide human society into two camps—the trustees of the immanent community of mankind and those who stand in its way. Thus there are moral imperatives in international relations whereby the actions of states enjoin not coexistence and cooperation, but the overthrow of the system of states and its replacement by a cosmopolitan society. Rules that sustain coexistence among the states can be bypassed if the imperatives of the higher morality require.

We have argued elsewhere that the placement of Soviet theory in the Kantian tradition was, even before the advent of "new thinking," a rather uneasy fit,* with Soviet and Marxist theories of international relations clearly frustrating the attempts of Western theorists bold enough to try to relate them to Western theories.

To pinpoint the position in international relations in the West of a theory that slides easily from one tradition to another is difficult indeed. First, as with all Marxist theories, Soviet theory is always explicitly normative, containing two images of the world—one present, one future. These two images might appear consistent with various traditions of international relations. One—that of a future

*Kubálková and Cruickshank (1985, 1989: 14ff.).

stateless world society—is an obligatory part of the credo of all Marxists because the achievement of communism ("emancipation" in Western Marxisms) is Marxism's defining feature. Communism is, in terms of our continuum, a Marxist version of a world society. It is the "ought to," that is, in contrast with the second image— namely, the description of the world as it is here and now. The long- and short-term policies (so-called strategies and tactics) are devised for spanning the distance between now and the future. Commitment to the final goal of a communist world society has remained the main ideological axiom throughout Soviet history. With the second image—the understanding of the world here and now—the strategies and tactics of transition and the perceived distance from the goal of communism change from one stage to the next.

Thus the early years of Stalinist "socialism in one country" represented a reluctant acknowledgement of the USSR's existence inside a hostile system of states. As we have noted, "new thinkers" interpret Lenin's well-known assertion about now living in a system of states (Piadyshev in "Perestroika" 1988: 7) as an indication of his awareness of an incipient interdependence in the gradual progression of Soviet theories of international relations along the continuum from the early nihilist belief in the possibility of the autarkic existence of the USSR, unconnected to other states. Khrushchev's doctrine of peaceful coexistence of "states of different socioeconomic systems" represented a further advance along the continuum insofar as it revealed an understanding of the world as a nascent international society.* That advance was made on the basis of the realization that, because of an increasingly more favorable "correlation of forces," the world was becoming a much more friendly gathering of states for the USSR, which, in light of the commonly perceived threat of nuclear annihilation, was in a position to devise some of the rules and institutions for the achievement of nuclear peace.

Despite its continuity with previous ideology in theoretical terms, "new thinking" departs significantly from earlier theories. It reaffirms beyond any doubt the commitment to the achievement of communist world society, but it lengthens substantially our distance from that goal and offers a new perception of the world as it is now. In terms of the continuum of the integration of states, the world has

*Cf. Kubálková and Cruickshank (1985: 28).

been quite unexpectedly declared a world society (Gorbachev 1986a: passim). "New thinking" represents the culmination of Soviet travel along the path of the continuum. Instead of the unifying impetus of modernity, or the incremental strengthening of shared values, Gorbachev and the "new thinkers" discover the integrative impulse of the world society in the exposure to a common threat resulting from the volatile mix of nuclear armed states in mutual contact—that is to say, in the interdependence of humanity's survival in a nuclear world. Shakhnazarov leaves us in no doubt as to the reasoning: the world has become a "world society because of the global problems" (1988a: 23). "New thinking," then, is not only supposed to capture the initial moment of the integrative traumatization, but also to be the vehicle by which the process of establishing the world society can advance.

"New Thinking": World Society

In a recent study by Izyumov and Kortunov (1988), there is an extraordinarily candid self-analysis of the weakness and failure of Soviet strategy in the Third World. It portrays a steadily weakening superpower which, aside from its military and space technology, barely reaches the level of development of a Third World country, and is therefore unlikely in the foreseeable future to reach the state of modernity or become instrumental in leading the world into the stage of world society. With its straitened economy and tattered image as a superpower, the Soviet Union has taken what seems to be the only avenue for initiative in international relations open to it—namely, to be the first to declare the existence of a world society, thereby enabling it to establish its global intellectual ascendancy.

The thrust of "new thinking" toward world society is in two directions. The first involves the strengthening of the existing core of a "common world culture," a process that seems at present to be defined by a rejection of Western "old" thinking in regard to justification of the states-system. It is rejected on the grounds that it ignores the existence of global values in favor of *cuius regio eius religio*—an international order based on power, with minimal rules of procedure which amount to no more than agreed ways of disagreeing (cf. Kortunov 1988). "New thinking" repudiates all aspects of the Western strategic doctrine of mutual deterrence or "balance of terror," and in so doing converges with the sophisticated arguments by Western critics of power realism.* The second direction of "new thinking's" thrust toward world society is the rejection of the Kantian idea of perpetual peace because it, like the Soviets' own earlier doctrine of peaceful coexistence, still provides for the unacceptable notion of subordinating peace to other values—to nationalism and the class struggle respectively.

It is regrettable that Western theorists of international relations do not read Gorbachev and other "new thinkers." As a result, they may be missing a historic event which, with hindsight, could well bear comparison in significance with the enunciation by Woodrow Wilson of his Fourteen Points. The Soviet Union has declared that the world has reached that high point of international relations theory—world society. This "upstaging" has not only theoretical but also political significance: it means that Soviet understanding of the nature of the "common planetary home" is "ahead of" the understanding of the West. "World Society," a Soviet theorist says, "is a historical category with real substance in the nuclear age for the first time" (Morozov 1986: 6).

It can be argued that on numerous occasions in the past Western theorists have argued along similar lines only to find themselves isolated and labelled utopian or idealist. The crucial difference, however, is that Soviet authors are not simply other utopian idealists who, in hailing the onset of the world society, are simply attacking the dominant Western paradigm of power realism. Soviet writers do not write as individual scholars, but on behalf of a Kantian "rational state" which can translate thought into policies. In the hands of Soviet leaders, "new thinking" is presented as a blueprint for the salvation of humanity.

The boldly visionary (and obviously premature) declaration of the world's arrival at the stage of world society necessitates equally bold changes in Soviet historical materialism. Certain anticipated developments have to be postponed, others advanced, and a number of its postulates must be redefined.

---

*Cf. the theoretical critique of power realism compiled in Robert O. Keohane, ed., *Neorealism and Its Critics* (New York: Columbia University Press, 1986).

"World Society" in the Context of Marxist Historical Materialism

The extraordinary tenacity of capitalism, pronounced over a century ago by Marx to be geriatric and dying, is now readily acknowledged, and the coexistence of socialism and capitalism is expected to span an entire epoch, lasting into the indefinite future. Where Khrushchev in the late 1950s foresaw the attainment of communism and capitalism's collapse in the 1980s, Shakhazarov envisages a time frame of another fifty years that takes us into the twenty-first century, around the year 2030 (Shakhnazarov 1984). Others posit an even more distant date, but most "new thinkers" (including by now even Shakhazarov) hesitate to commit themselves to a time. There is also the fact that the nuclear danger advances "ahead of schedule" that Marxist universalism that was so downplayed in earlier Soviet Marxism-Leninism that Western commentators mistook its reappearance as a sign of the demise of Marxism. The argument now is easy to follow: if the deterioration into nuclear war is not firmly checked and the threat removed for all time, the world society of communism might never materialize. The achievement of world communism, previously assumed to be historically preordained, is now recognized to have become radically contingent.

There has already been one important casualty of "new thinking's" rearrangement of historical materialism: the theory of imperialism on which Soviet Marxist-Leninist theories have always been grounded has had to be discreetly shelved. "New thinking" disconnects entities that Bukharin and Lenin in their theory of imperialism tied together—namely, the capitalist mode of production and the states-system. According to "new thinking," war is the danger of nuclear extinction, and unlike tenets in the theory of imperialism is held to derive not from capitalism but from capitalist *states*. Capitalism as a mode of production has produced the weapons, but it is the capitalist states-system that is to be blamed for the brinkmanship over the years. Thus the root source of the present predicament of humanity is the capitalist states-system, with the socialist states as reluctant participants. Even in the discussion recently opened in the spirit of glasnost, one Soviet writer after another rejects the idea of equal responsibility for international conflict or the arms race. Like dangerous toys and a naughty child, capitalism, which as a

mode of production yields the murderous weapons, has to be separated from a states-system that avails itself of them. Writer after
writer rejects the Clausewitzian notion, adapted by Marxists and by
Lenin in particular, and with it the idea of war as a continuation of
class-based state policies. For the same reason the meaning of peaceful coexistence had to be changed by removing the reference to class
struggle from the original "peaceful coexistence of states of different
socioeconomic systems as *a form of class struggle*" (our italics) as
described at the 20th CPSU Congress by Khrushchev. The linkage of
state politics to class struggle was dropped from the proposition in
Gorbachev's political report to the 27th CPSU Congress.

It is this separation of international politics from class struggle
that Soviet writers refer to as the "de-ideologization" of international
relations, as distinct from the common Western understanding of
giving up ideology altogether. The ideological conflict is to be shifted
elsewhere. As Soviet writers explain: "Interstate relations in general
cannot be the sphere in which the fate of the confrontation between
world socialism and world capitalism is decided" (Primakov 1987:
3). Or alternatively, "revolution will come in conditions of peace. . . .
Communism will win but the forms are not certain" (Plimak 1987:
87). One thing that does seem certain to the Soviet writers is that
"new thinking," by outlining the existence of global problems, calls
for a "change in the center of gravity in the revolutionary movement"
(*ibid.*).

The thrust of "new thinking" as a critique of power realism lies
in its deemphasis of the states-system. Indeed it might be construed
as a strategy for that system's demise. The portrait it paints is of a
world from which the states-system fades into obscurity: it is a world
with a heterogeneous socioeconomic foundation of a great plurality
of communities. Soviet commentators keep returning to the theme
that the prolonged, albeit antagonistic, coexistence of capitalism and
socialism is a given; they speak of "capitalists and socialists," avoid-
ing mention of "capitalist and socialist states." Over this socioeconomic substructure there arches a superstructure which has (in the
Soviet view) all the initial requisites of a world society: an all-human
morality and a hierarchy of values headed by peace, reflecting the
right and responsibility of every individual to live on the planet as
his/her common home. The humanism that is clearly present in
classical Marxism, but was lost sight of in Soviet Leninist-Stalinist

orthodoxy, is brought to the surface. As Engels promised, states will wither away, but no longer as an immediate consequence of the demise of capitalism. With the causal relation turned around, the withering away of states becomes a precondition of that demise. International politics will begin the process of eclipsing states by focusing on the reconciliation of the global all-human level with that of the individual: "I think," says Gorbachev, "that the most important is Man."

"New Thinking" and International Law

The most important feature of the superstructure of the new world society is obviously "new thinking" itself. It contains the new all-human moral code which will be the driving force both of the further development of the global superstructure and of Soviet foreign policy. According to the "new thinkers," the basic institutions that reflect this new vision already exist in rudimentary form: they refer to those parts of international law that enshrine such concepts as the "common heritage of mankind" and lay stress on the "democratic" forums of multilateral diplomacy—most particularly the UN General Assembly—up to and including their law-making and law-interpreting functions.* Both Soviet and Third World jurists have been describing these for some time as "new," and they precede in "newness" other aspects of the global superstructure. Since "new international law" arrived well before "new thinking," it is argued by some Soviet writers that "the legal foundation of World Society is [already] formed" (Morozov 1986: 9).

One of the swiftest and most successful invasions ever staged by the Soviets has no doubt been Gorbachev's move into the Grotian tradition of international relations along the lines discussed earlier in this chapter. Unlike the broadly based discussion set in train by the general idea of "new thinking," commentaries on such subjects as international law and international organizations have been the preserve of members of an inner circle, with the delivery of major

---

*J. N. Hazard, "International Law under Contemporary Pressures," *Military Law Review* 83 (Winter 1979); V. Kubálková and A. A. Cruickshank, "Marxism, International Law and International Organizations," in Kubálková and Cruickshank (1985, 1989: 158ff.).

statements reserved mainly for Gorbachev and his foreign minister. Comment is also made by other officials in the Foreign Ministry, such as Petrovsky, and by such "gurus" as Shakhnazarov, but the writing on international law is less prolific, and the "new thinkers'" definitive statement on the subject ("New Doctrine of International Law") came in Gorbachev's article addressed to the UN General Assembly and published in *Pravda* (16 September 1987) and other Soviet journals. Shevardnadze's (1988c) address to the General Assembly a year later reiterates Gorbachev's major propositions— further strengthened by Gorbachev in his UN address later that year. Of the several commentaries on both of these speeches, the most prescient is Shakhnazarov's article "Governability of the World," published both in *Pravda* (1988a) and *International Affairs* (1988b). Further insight into proposed changes in international law as the fundamental element of "new thinking" is to be found in a variety of documents issued from the General Assembly's 41st, 42nd, and 43rd sessions or in extracts from proposals put out at the time by the Soviets or by East Europeans on their behalf. From these sources—and once again from Gorbachev's political report to the 27th Congress—two key concepts emerge: the concept of "balance of interests" and the concept of a "comprehensive system of security."

Western Responses to Soviet Initiatives in International Law

Because of their importance to the overall structure of "new thinking," the reactions of Western commentators to the new Soviet approach to international law and organization merit separate discussion. The most common Western response corresponds to the standard Western interpretation of "new thinking" generally in its assumption that the USSR's long ideological connection with Marxism has at last been severed. Anders Aslund regards Gorbachev's September 1987 *Pravda* article as "remarkable for its lack of ideological rhetoric and [for its] constructive spirit"—a genuine attempt on Gorbachev's part to "enhance multilateral diplomacy" (1988: 27). Sestanovich echoes that view, crediting Gorbachev with the freeing of Soviet policy from ideological preconceptions and constraints (1988a: 5).

Aslund goes on to welcome Gorbachev's concern for "economic security," for his desire to build a new economic world order with the easing of the debt burden of the developing world as a first step, and for his perception of the need to abolish protectionist barriers. Another Western commentator thought Gorbachev's proposals in the same article were "startling" and "stunning" (Chace 1988: 9), and Gorbachev's new-found interest in ecological and environmental problems was generally met with expressions of pleasant surprise. Against this background it might be noted that Primakov, one of "new thinking's" Soviet luminaries, commented that Gorbachev's article contained "the quintessence of ideas that enable one to understand the new Soviet approaches to world problems" (1987a: 15).

In an article published in the influential *Problems of Communism*, Sestanovich, commenting on Shevardnadze's address to the United Nations (which developed points from Gorbachev's earlier statements), finds the notion of the Soviet Union seeking a world peace maintained "exclusively" by the United Nations and its Security Council difficult to understand. It is "extraordinary" and "not to be taken seriously" because it would mean the "demobilization" of Soviet foreign policy. In Sestanovich's view, "certain Soviet officials have pushed 'new thinking' outlandishly far. One should keep in mind that in the age of 'glasnost' many statements, even by those in high positions, are probably not authoritative" (1988a: 6). Shakhnazarov's article on the "Governability of the World," which in our view does not simply "embellish" [Sestanovich's word] but enlarges on the idea of "balance of interests," is found by Sestanovich to have also badly missed the mark and to be unrepresentative of the official view. Neither Gorbachev, his foreign minister, nor the president of the Soviet Association of Political Scientists and Gorbachev's aide (Sestanovich would have us understand) are abreast of the "true" direction of Soviet thinking, which, as in the past, has been the task of Western commentators to determine. The reason he advances now for dismissing interpretations by Soviet writers is, oddly enough, glasnost.

Concrete Proposals: International Law and Organizations

Just how "non-ideological" and "stunning" are these proposals by Gorbachev to have earned such lavish Western praise? According to Gorbachev, existing international mechanisms and institutions are the "bricks" with which a start can be made on building security into the system of the future. He has made the gesture of repaying a Soviet debt of $200 million in back dues to the United Nations to enable a fresh start to be made on the foundation of what Shevardnadze is now moved to describe as "our house of peace." It is now the "main work unit" and the "heart" of the "universal international alliance" that "must rise above differences, which, to quote Albert Einstein, are infinitely small compared to the danger that threatens us all" (Shevardnadze 1988a: 2) "I do not venture to foretell how the system would appear in its final form," says Gorbachev in inviting the drawing up of a commission to take charge of "restructuring."

The overall aim of all Soviet or East European proposals to initiate "restructuring" is "openness"* and the "democratization" of international relations. They are referred to as part of a package designated by the Soviets as a "comprehensive international security system." The Soviet proposals have incorporated all the recommendations of the Palme Commission and of a subsequent UN comprehensive study on concepts of security. Soviet representatives took part in the preparation of both of these.† Part of the package goes beyond the security measures recommended by the Palme Commission to encompass economic, humanitarian, ecological, and information concerns. The "comprehensive security system" purports to offer an answer to the "global problems of mankind" and implements the salient security features of the concept of "new thinking" as we have identified them. Inasmuch as the main form of implementation of "new thinking's" precepts is through proposals to

*TASS, 2 November 1988; FBIS-SOV-88-215, 7 November 1988.

†The report, entitled "Common Security," was prepared by the Palme Commission (after its chairman, Olaf Palme of Sweden), and submitted to the General Assembly in 1982. In 1984 and 1985, the Secretary-General, with the assistance of a multinational team of experts representing Algeria, Argentina, Australia, China, the German Democratic Republic, India, the Philippines, Romania, Sweden, Uganda, the USSR, Venezuela, and Yugoslavia carried out a comprehensive study of concepts of security. By Resolution 40/94E, adopted without voting, the General Assembly accepted the recommendations of the study.

change international organizations and international law, clearly the concept falls into the category of legalist-moralist theories associated with the Grotian approach to international relations.

In applying "new thinking" to international politics, Gorbachev insists on the "primacy of international law" in a process summarized by Shevardnadze as a progression from "states of law to a world of law." In terms of its sources, it is a much more broadly conceived international law than previously recognized by the Soviets. Hitherto the Soviets, in company with the Third World, have rejected custom as a source of international law, but this is no longer the case. Socialist and Third World members of the UN have combined their efforts to strengthen the legal standing and force of documents adopted by the General Assembly, and modifying the content of the "general international law" is also on their agenda. The latter, referred to by the Soviets as the "international law of peaceful coexistence," is now seen to play a highly progressive role. It applies to the countries of the socialist bloc except where it contravenes the provisions of "socialist international law."

Gorbachev confirms the trend toward the creation of a new international law, and in doing so he "emphatically stress[es] the need for making the status of important political documents passed at the UN by consensus more binding morally and politically"—a view endorsed by Shevardnadze in his address to the 43rd session of the General Assembly (1988c). The objective is to make the Charter of Economic Rights and important disarmament documents passed by the UN fully accepted parts of international law. This would mean that the UN resolutions endorsing the Soviet and East European proposals to proceed with the establishment of a comprehensive security system* (approved by the 42nd and 43rd sessions of the General Assembly by overwhelming majorities) would carry more than moral force. Gorbachev regards the degree of consensus reached in the adoption of these resolutions as indication of the "new mode of thinking and actions of states" and evidence of the "trend towards the democratization of international relations . . . gaining momentum."

---

*Resolution 41/92 (12-4-1986) of the 41st session of the UN General Assembly, drafted by socialist countries, proposed to establish a comprehensive security system in military-political, economic, humanitarian, and ecological areas (102 votes in favor).

In the view of Soviet writers, the resolution for a comprehensive security system provides a framework for a new "restructuring of international relations." As they now point out, the absence of war (to which the USSR has now committed itself as the "highest human value") is not an end in itself: there is a need to make provision for a comprehensive system of international security, and to that end the UN should draft a new document (revise the charter of the UN?) to strengthen its role (Fyodorov 1988: 9). According to Shevardnadze, the essence of the "entirely new system of international security" is the provision of a set of nonmilitary guarantees—technical, political, economic, and humanitarian—elevating trust and peaceful coexistence to the status of basic principles of international relations (cited in *ibid.*, 93). Soviet leaders speak of the new international relations as "civilized" (Gorbachev 1987e)—an allusion not only to Lenin's notion of "civilized cooperation," but also to the historical exclusion of the colonies (now become the 100-plus Third World countries) from the reach of international law on the grounds that they were lacking in "civilization." The Soviets have turned the tables by using the "not civilized" label to describe the military-based relations which are the basis of the "old" outmoded thinking of the West.

The fact that it is the role of the General Assembly which is to be enhanced is obscured by Soviet calls for a greater role to be assigned also to the Security Council—an intention spelled out both by Gorbachev and his foreign minister. Gorbachev proposes that the members of the Security Council be designated guarantors of regional security, and that a "hot line" be opened between the UN headquarters, the members of the Security Council, and the chairman of the Non-Aligned Movement. He believes the Security Council and General Assembly should lead the way, but should avail themselves of the services of the International Court of Justice to encourage more widespread acceptance of its jurisdiction. Shevardnadze has suggested the drafting of a code of crimes against peace and the security of mankind as a major step in the implementation of "new thinking." Interestingly, in an interview following the signing of the Delhi Declaration, Gorbachev mentioned power realism, with its notions of balance of power, national interest, and the like, as an example of the dangerous thoughts and stereotypes that should be internationally proscribed.

Further Soviet proposals include the creation of a UN naval force, the strengthening of a number of international organizations and UN specialized agencies such as the International Atomic Energy Agency, the creation of a number of new agencies (such as a world space agency), the revitalization of UNESCO, the establishment of a consultative council under UN auspices that would bring together the world's intellectual elite, and the establishment of a "new information order" which would contribute to the spreading of mutual trust among states and inhibit the dissemination of such ideas as the "Soviet threat."

"Balance of Interests"

The concept at the center of this new vision of international relations (according to Soviet writers) is "balance of interests"—a particularly apt phrase that simultaneously evokes and challenges the concept of "balance of power," the centerpiece of the "old thinking." It is used in conjunction with the Soviet concepts of comprehensive security system and world society, and Gorbachev himself contrasts the concept of balance of interests with balance of power and with the militaristic doctrine on which the policy of force rests (1986a). Shakhnazarov explains that balance of interests refers to a "new international political order of coordinating interests of sovereign states"—not to a world state, but to an "international body based on a voluntary agreement between states, including states belonging to different social and political systems." Shakhnazarov admits that such a system is as yet not in existence, and it will require work to bring about its realization, but it points in the right direction (1988a: 19). As Gorbachev puts it, the "idea of a comprehensive system of security is the first plan for a possible new organization of life in our common planetary home" (1986a: 11). In this context he recognizes the UN as one of the existing bricks in a world that "increasingly needs a mechanism capable of discussing common problems . . . [while] searching for a balance of differing, contradictory, yet real, interests of the contemporary community of states and nations" (3).

The logic of the Soviet argument is not always easy to follow, but that does not mean that there is no logic. Torn from the context of Soviet pronouncements, balance of interests has already been erroneously interpreted as meaning Soviet readiness to "sacrifice some of its traditional interests" (Sestanovich 1988a: 6) and received as evidence of a new Soviet willingness to compromise and accept "asymmetries." The Soviets' own logic, gleaned from the context of Soviet writing, suggests otherwise. Without that logic there are some statements made by Soviet leaders which appear in the next breath to have been significantly qualified or modified. Sestanovich notes that Soviet proposals to strengthen the UN and other international organizations would mean limitations on the sovereignty of states. Indeed Shevardnadze implies as much ("Let there be no lament . . . over sacred national prerogatives" [1988c]), but he hastens to dispel any concern that the Soviet Union is headed toward one-worldism by adding that "freedom of choice" is the linchpin of "new thinking." It would seem, then, that when the Soviets suggest a coexisting plurality of sovereign states, the states would be sovereign in name only because they are to be progressively disarmed. Such coexisting states would partake of that interdependence which, according to Shakhnazarov (1988b), equates with being "governable." In the changed circumstances of the present-day world, he explains, when the Soviet Union is no longer isolated (gauged by the frequency of its initiatives winning majority votes in the General Assembly), it does not have to oppose one-worldism. In some areas (aviation, posts and communications, etc.) the global arrangements are already of a confederal nature. Shakhnazarov notes a trend toward what he refers to as a "world concert" based on a surrender of sovereignty that calls for no lamentations because the only sovereignty that matters is that of the people's will; he likens the future world concert to an orchestra without a conductor. Claiming that with this idea of no one in charge Shakhnazarov has gone too far, Alexander Bovin stresses the continuing contradictory and class nature of the world. Our reading of Shakhnazarov suggests that he is referring to a more distant condition of the world society when he anticipates consensus will be reached by the leaderless "orchestra," which bears distinct similarities both to Karl Deutsch's world of pluralistic security communities and to the future society of world communism.

   Western scholars of international law have long been aware of a pronounced tendency in Soviet legal doctrine toward one-worldism. It would seem it has now also reached Soviet attitudes toward international organizations and their approach to international politics generally. The progression begins with the gradual disarmament of states by stages, culminating in the outlawing of international violence and the possession of weapons (both defensive and offensive). Beyond that Soviet writers emphasize the need to investigate the implications of diversity, national and cultural, in a world made up of nonsovereign societies. Such lines of investigation have indeed an extended lineage in Marxist thought. The Austro-Marxist Otto Bauer, for example, suggested that national and cultural diversity and plurality could develop fully only in a flourishing communist world society without sovereign states.*

When the Soviets insist that their proposals do not threaten the sovereignty of states, they are speaking of sovereignty in a restricted sense—as the embodiment of the "will of the people." Essential to an understanding of the Soviet view is the Marxist messianism and universalism referred to earlier, for they clearly underpin Gorbachev's declaration of the coincidence of Soviet and global interests: "Our state interests are not at variance with the interests of the peoples or of the masses of working people in any society" (1986a: 10). In light of such declarations, the concepts of balance of interests and world concert show up rather differently.

Envisaged in the Soviet world of the future is a shift from the realist balance of *power* to the Soviet notion of balance of *interests*, taking us from the nineteenth-century "concert of Europe" to Shakhnazarov's less ethnocentric world concert. These terminological parallels, with "new thinking" and old thinking in apposition, can be seen as part of the attack on the old thinking of power realism. The terminology is chosen to imply anarchical, acephalous political organization "without a conductor"—imagery that will dispel fears of the traditionally assumed Soviet intentions to create a world state. In the Soviet vision there will be no. central government in the future political arrangement of the world; it will, however, be a world society inasmuch as it is characterized by globally shared values that allow the balance of interests to function.

Die Nationalitätenfrage und die Sozialdemokratie (Vienna: Wiener Volksbuchhandlung, 1907).

From "Balance of Power" to "Balance of Interests"?

What then of interstate relations, with barriers lowered and the constraints of state sovereignty set aside by Soviet "new thinking"? What of the states-system itself—that *bête noire* of Marx whose "feudal excrescence" was until recently defended in Soviet theories of international relations as a bulwark against capitalism?

With "new thinking" the Soviets return to Marx, and part of the rediscovered common ground has to do with the states-system. According to the "new thinkers," contrary to previous expectations, the demise of the states-system will no longer coincide with that of capitalism, with which for the period of imperialism it had merged. The states-system will now precede capitalism into oblivion. We have already remarked that, although capitalism continues to be seen as the source of conflict, it is the capitalist states-system that is seen as the source of military engagements and nuclear confrontations. Capitalism can be handled in a cooperative, interdependent relationship so long as it is disarmed—an emasculated capitalism which will make available the technology (particularly the information technology) necessary to ensure the ascendancy of the future collectivist (not to use the discredited word *communist*) world society. The next (and final) stage of the historically inevitable struggle between capitalism and socialism will take place in the absence of sovereign armed states. Indeed the withering away of sovereign states is now seen as an essential precondition of the joining of the final battle. The two fronts—that is, the class struggle, or the historical confrontation between capitalism and socialism as modes of production, on the one hand, and the struggle between states on the other hand—are clearly separated from each other.

This change is portrayed as beneficial to socialist historical development. First, "the goals of development are unattainable without access to the achievements of present-day technical civilization, which means interaction with the epicentres of capitalism" (Pankin 1988: 14). Second, once the conflict of states is moved on the historical agenda ahead of the conflict between socialist and capitalist modes of production, the Soviet Union can join forces with all the non-Marxists worldwide opposed to the states-system and to power realism.

Their common front is "new thinking," and their attack on power realism is frontal. Historical materialism has always represented a rejection and repudiation of power realism, but the "new thinking," by availing itself of the arguments of the non-Marxist critique, gives its repudiation a keener edge. The advocates of historical materialism have always denied the validity of major propositions of power realism,* specifically that (1) nation-states have been the most important actors in world history, (2) there is a sharp distinction between domestic and international politics, (3) states are unitary and rational actors, (4) the aim of interstate relations is a quest for peace/security/order† (despite the recent redefinition of peace in "new thinking," Soviet writers still argue that permanent peace cannot be achieved within the context of international relations), and (4) the framework in which sovereign states operate is anarchic. For this reason alone, the traditional framework is no longer tolerable.

The main processes that "new thinking" prescribes are believed to be already in train. They are twofold: first, the moral condemnation of national interests by humanity as a whole, and second, internationalization of national interests into global needs and interests. National interests will still be pursued, but without the power element.

The Soviet concept of security spelled out in "new thinking" (points 5–8 in our list of ten points) is an important initial part of this process. The overall implication of these points for international relations theory is that states are declared morally and geopolitically obsolete because they can no longer provide security for their citizens. According to "new thinking," security can now be conceived only on the global level—no longer on the level of states, not even the most powerful. The idea that security is attainable only as a global goal is considered so unassailable by "new thinkers" that around it revolves their critique of power realism, with its stereotypes of balance of power, balance of terror, military superiority, bipolarism, and all the other concepts alleged to be outmoded.

---

*Assembled from J. Vasquez, *The Power of Power Politics* (London: Frances Pinter, 1983), and R. O. Keohane, "Theory of World Politics: Structural Realism and Beyond," in *Neorealism and Its Critics*, ed. Keohane (New York: Columbia University Press, 1986).

†See K. Holsti, *The Dividing Discipline: Hegemony and Diversity in International Theory* (London: Allen and Unwin, 1985).

Power realism—runs the argument—extrapolates from the pre-nuclear past patterns that are no longer applicable to the changed historical circumstances of the present. Accordingly, the new doctrine of comprehensive security elaborated in Soviet writing envisages the gradual erosion of state sovereignty and the negation of the deterrence system. To bring about this systemic change, the stress is to be on security by political methods alone through multilateral diplomacy and decisions in international forums. The process of erosion of states needs to be helped along not only by a restructuring of international organizations at the highest levels, but also by the actions and attitudes of every individual. As Kortunov explains: "Traditional morality teaches that it is impossible to be a patriot and at the same time sharply criticize one's country's policy. Nuclear-age morality teaches that a patriot must critically assess the policy of his state" (1988: 145). The stress is on the conversion of every individual to "new thinking" as the only avenue remaining along which to make further advance.

Accompanying the globalization of national interests in "new thinking," there takes place—in the reverse direction—the "nationalization" of the revolutionary advance. That which in Lenin's theory of imperialism was elevated to the international level is now returned to where Marx located it—*inside* societies. It is there, and not through wars that involve states, that the transformation of capitalism will take place. The contradiction between socialism and capitalism will be resolved on the basis of peaceful coexistence, economic competition, and ideological struggle—i.e., ultimately in the battle for the mind of each individual seen now as waged between old and new thinking.

The concept of capitalism coexisting with communism in a world society defined by the absence of sovereign states is certainly new, and by classical Marxist standards an impossibility, if not a contradiction in terms. Similarly it can be argued that "new thinking" as a theory of international relations is a self-contradictory mishmash of notions hastily brought together to confirm Gorbachev's recognition of the Soviet need for a theoretical breakthrough. This is a not too cynical reading, especially in light of the current stampede of Soviet academics to the United States. "New thinking" can also be described as an unrealistic response to an exaggerated description of the predicament of mankind in the nuclear age—as another idealist, utopian, legalist-moralist approach to the study of international relations. Or it can be argued that "Gorbachev genuinely cares for mankind," but beyond that the processes described in "new thinking" and its perception of the world have little or no substance. As for the impact of "new thinking" on Western studies of international relations, it may supplement pressures already at work for the reinstatement of some of the normative issues that were prominent in the early stages of the discipline's development, but on its showing to date "new thinking" stands as little chance against realism as did its idealist predecessors.

Beyond these findings it could be added that *as a theory* "new thinking" does not merit further consideration, and that when it concedes that the states-system so overshadows Marxism's traditional concerns as to put them in the background until the conflicts of interstate politics are somehow resolved, it refutes its own arguments against power realism. The cutting edge of Marxist analysis could be said to have lost some of its keenness through too long a contact with the states-system, obliging it to fall back on non-Marxist positions to reinforce its criticisms.

The intellectual superiority of power realism can furthermore be seen in the fact that "new thinking" is easily explained in power realist terms. There is nothing new in "new thinking's" commitment to destroy the states-system: the Soviet Union has never been short of theories in this regard. The only difference now is that the USSR is beset by daunting domestic problems at a time when its superpower status in the states-system is problematical. Conceivably, then, "new thinking" is nothing more than propaganda—a sort of disinformation devised to gain respite from the high-profile, resource-consuming posture the Soviets must maintain in order to keep up with the United States in the arms/space race and the eyes of the Third World. Many Sovietologists use this power realist argument when they specify the needs of perestroika as the main source of "new thinking. If this explanation is valid, "new thinking" may as well be returned to the library shelves to join the other abandoned displays of Soviet "thinking."

The Logic of "New Thinking" as a Marxist Theory

To dismiss "new thinking" because of its weakness vis-à-vis the old thinking of power realism, and/or because it is merely another example of an idealist, utopian, moralist-legalist approach to international relations, would be ill-advised. We are, after all, not dealing with a Karl Deutsch or a Woodrow Wilson. "New thinking" is the theoretical core of the state ideology of a Marxist superpower. As Aspaturian puts it, whether Soviet thought is superior or inferior to Western academic analyses is almost totally irrelevant because they do not have the same relationship to state power that Marxism-Leninism does.* Soviet "new thinking" has to be viewed not only as a theory of international relations, but also as a Marxist framework for the implementation of Soviet foreign policy. It is with good reason that Soviet writers insist that it is "new thinking" that mainly drives their foreign policy—not perestroika, or not only perestroika—and it is in this regard that the study of "new thinking" is important.

At a minimum the analysis of "new thinking" points the direction of the new foreign policy approaches that will guide Soviet action. The initiatives in regard to international law and international organization assume a totally different appearance when we no longer see them as a mere variant of the Grotian approach to international politics. The new Soviet foreign policy is fully consistent with "new thinking" interpreted as a Marxist state ideology, albeit one with a new array of tactical options.

In this context it might be worth noting that many Western critics of power realism insist that knowledge (including presumably "new thinking") is constitutive of certain relations of power. This is particularly true of the British, American, and Canadian writers of the "critical" school,[†] who contend that ideas, ideologies, and worldviews can play influential roles in international relations in profound ways.

Thus the notion that ideas can be used as effectively as weapons in international relations has a lineage in Western thought. "New thinking" itself provides a good example if we are prepared to see it not only as an attempt at redefinition of the Soviet understanding of international relations, but also as a program for action by a Marxist superpower. "New thinking," then, is not only an attempt to devise a new Marxist theory of international relations, but the meaning and logic of "new thinking" can be explained in Marxist

*V. Aspaturian, *Power and Process in Soviet Foreign Policy* (Boston: Little, Brown, 1971).

†See footnote p. 110–11 below.

terms. Turned around in this sense it approximates Gramsci's revolutionary *strategy of counter-hegemony*. We conclude this chapter by outlining Gramsci's ideas as they appear to us to relate to "new thinking."

"Grotian Marxism": Antonio Gramsci

The approach closest to the Grotian tradition in the annals of Marxist thought is that of Gramsci. The work of Gramsci, extremely popular in Western social science a decade or so ago, in the 1980s attracts considerable attention both from Soviet philosophers and from "critical" international relations writers. Some Western theorists (R. W. Cox, in particular) have extended Gramsci's thinking to the status of a theory of international relations.* Although Cox's Gramscian theory of international relations does not aim at either an explanation of Soviet politics or of "new thinking," it makes such an explanation plausible. In the Soviet view, Gramsci's ideas are consistent with Lenin's work (in which they are seen to have been anticipated), and he provides new tactics for the implementation of Lenin's goals. To Soviet thinkers Gramsci's "historicism" refers to his skill in applying abstract Marxist-Leninist notions to specific historical circumstances.†

Gramsci did not write on international relations, nor could he have anticipated the Soviet predicament fifty years later. His thinking

---

*See R. W. Cox: "Gramsci, Hegemony and International Relations: An Essay in Method," *Millennium* 12, 2 (1983), and "Social Forces, States and World Orders: Beyond International Relations Theory," *Millennium* 10, 2 (1981). For an attempt to explain Soviet domestic perestroika as the creation and cultivation of selected elements of Gramscian civil society in the Soviet Union (grassroots democracy at the micro-societal level to activate the human element and substitute the capitalist drive for profit), see Bialer (1987: 65).

†M. N. Greckij, "Gramshi i sovremennost" [Gramsci and the present], *Voprosy filosofii* 4 (1987): 114; see also G. Smirnov, *Antonio Gramshi*, Izbr. Proizv. [Antonio Gramsci, collected works], (Moscow, 1980); V. S. Grinko, "Problema cheloveka v rabotakh Antonio Gramshi" [The problem of man in the world of Antonio Gramsci], *Filosofskie nauki* 2 (1983); S. Matveev, "Problemy vzaimosviazi politiki, kultury i mirovozrenia v 'Tjuremnykh tetradiakh' A. Gramshi" [Problems of relations of politics, culture and worldview in the *Prison Notebooks* of A. Gramsci], *Filosofskie nauki* 6 (1985).

is relevant to present Soviet circumstances because one of his theories—the theory of counter-hegemony—was devised as a rationale of defeat and a strategy of failure, much like "new thinking." Gramsci conceived his concept of hegemony to explain the failure of revolutions in Western Europe and, by implication, everywhere other than tsarist Russia. "In pre-revolutionary Russia," Gramsci writes, "the state was everything"; it was the "fortress" itself. In contrast, in Western Europe the state is to Gramsci but "an outer ditch" within which lies the inner fortress of "civil society," which is no longer based exclusively on violence and coercion, but on hegemonic consensus created by a variety of cultural and ideological instruments.* Gramsci's hegemony, as applied to the international level by Cox, can be interpreted as "an order within the world economy expressed in the dominant mode of production supporting universal norms, international institutions, and mechanisms for the behaviour of states and other actors."† Instrumental in the creation of the hegemonic consensus is the "historical bloc," which consists of bourgeois intellectuals.

Soviet theory has regarded Gramsci as "one of its own," occupying an honored place in the Leninist intellectual tradition. As M. N. Greckij observes, Gramsci's tactics are worthy of emulation as a creative application of abstract Leninist formulas. He stresses Gramsci's understanding of revolution as a protracted and arduous process that requires the complete transformation of life and society, not excluding man himself. To paraphrase Greckij on the subject of counter-hegemony (in our context read "new thinking"): the proletariat needs to take to heart the interests of others. Counter-hegemony consists of a broadening of interests, a cathartic cleansing of attitudes of indifference toward great social problems, an elimination of narrow economist lines of thinking, a rejection of the slavish replication of the patterns of others—i.e., the assumption of control.**

In the present circumstances the Gramscian strategy of anti-hegemony is the only sensible option for the USSR. The relative weakness of the Soviets puts their international relations role in doubt now and into the future. Its geopolitical gains in the Third World

*Cox (1981: 165ff.).

†*Ibid.*, 171–72.

**Greckij, p. 110.

cannot be maintained with any degree of permanence except through the use of overwhelming military might, but against such use (which became associated with and developed alongside the "fortress" of states-system) there are now persuasive arguments that warn both of new dangers of military involvement and of loss of face and prestige for anyone who would apply force. Such involvements have become prohibitively expensive for an economically overextended superpower that seeks to challenge the hegemony of an antagonist securely rooted in a capitalist mode of production.

It is not difficult to find direct evidence of Soviet thinking along Gramscian lines in recent Soviet writings. Both Scanlan and Bialer (1988) have noticed Gorbachev's Gramscian bent in regard to his domestic reform aimed at strengthening the civil society inside the Soviet Union.* In our view Gorbachev's reforms are aimed at three types of civil society (in the Gramscian sense): his own domestic civil society, Western civil society, and international civil society. In all three cases the idea is to create broad networks of non-political relations among individuals, groups, and states who voluntarily and independently carry out many social and economic functions and, in the international relations context, help promote Soviet foreign policies. The Soviets have a great deal to say about the new emphasis placed on all forms of social consciousness (Mshvenieradze 1986: 52) or the need for perestroika of the global as well as the Soviet consciousness (Kirshin 1987: 26). Gorbachev repeats his reliance on "the help of the intelligentsia" (1986a: 4), Shakhnazarov describes the process of the "internationalization of intellect" (1986: 23), and Dobrynin speaks of the need for efforts "further to develop and enrich Marxism-Leninism" by combining it with the "humanistic and general democratic ideals of all social forces seriously concerned for the preservation of humanity" (1986). These forces even include one of Gramsci's favorite allies in the original counter-hegemonic strategy—the church (Glagolev 1988: 60). Smirnov cites Marx's dictum that "ideas become a material force the moment they take hold of the masses" (1987: 15), and Soviet writers make no attempt to conceal their delight at the "unprecedented popularity of the USSR," citing with considerable satisfaction Western opinion polls that give

---

*"This is the vision of a new open society in the USSR—of a state held in check by vigorous social forces" (Scanlan 1988: 43).

Gorbachev a high popularity rating as a statesman and indicate declining concerns in Western populations about the Soviet threat (Gorbachev 1987f: 422; Primakov 1987: 4; etc.). Reducing fears of the Soviet threat—one of the first results of the "Gorbachev effect"—has become one of the top Soviet priorities.

In our view all signs point to the development of a new counter-hegemonic strategy designed neither to foster revolutions nor to wage wars. Such a strategy would put coercive mechanisms in the background without giving them up altogether. The Gramscian theory opens up a dimension of conflict and confrontation beyond the power realist use or threat of force. It recognizes a new type of weapon which the correlation-of-forces "gauge" might register as equivalent to SDI ("star wars"). A high diplomatic profile is an essential part of the counter-hegemonic strategy—one that projects an innovative, flexible, and altruistic image of the USSR. It requires the establishment of an intellectual ascendancy and points in the direction of a new reliance on superstructural elements such as international law, international organization, and propaganda. In the final analysis the thrust is toward influencing each individual mind to reject the economy/technology–powered military approach to the world in favor of the only revolutionary option realistically available to the Soviet Union in the 1980s and beyond.

The belated Soviet recognition of nuclear and other global dangers, and their discovery of the concept of "new thinking" at this time, begs for interpretation as part of the strategy of counter-hegemony. The concept is a collective product of both Soviet thinkers and Western intellectuals, which amounts in Gramscian terms to a new "historical bloc." On their shoulders is the task of creating the new consensus that will undermine the instruments of hegemony, including that of the states-system.

Viewed in this light, the impact of "new thinking" runs much deeper than ordinary propaganda, which has always occupied pride of place in Soviet ideology. As an instrument of a counter-hegemonic strategy, the reliance on the formation of ideas and their dissemination becomes much more profound, for not only does it fulfill the disinformation function associated with propaganda, but it becomes a precondition for political change. The concept of "new thinking," and the spread of ideas associated with it, will now be part of the correlation of forces for it aims at nothing less than the changing of people's minds about the nature of international relations, the nature of the United States, and particularly the nature of the Soviet Union through identification with the target societies' problems and values. It is through such identification and by cooption that change in the ideopolitical consensus along the lines drawn by Gramsci could be effected. In this regard Gramsci and "new thinking" converge with the Western Marxist notion of "emancipation," which in one of its meanings is an exhortation to think right, think new.* The sequence and timing of the theoretical elaboration of "new thinking" in the USSR also tends to bear out the validity of its explanation in Marxist Gramscian terms, challenging the proposition that all there is to "new thinking" is a desperate search for respite for Soviet domestic perestroika.

In the following chapter we try to discover to what extent "new thinking" will affect the charting of new foreign policy courses—whether, in other words, "new thinking" is the "methodology of action" that Gorbachev himself has claimed it to be (1987a).

---

*Paul Piccone; cited in R. Antonio, "The Origin, Development and Contemporary Status of Critical Theory," *Sociological Quarterly* 24 (1983): 326.

Chapter 5

"NEW THINKING" AS A
FOREIGN POLICY GUIDE

The wide-ranging Western assessments of the "Gorbachev phenomenon," the "Gorbachev effect," or Gorbachev's "new foreign
policy," which have become the preferred terms for "new thinking,"
reveal a degree of Western confusion and bewilderment. Most
Sovietologists agree that the USSR has already changed, but the
methodology of studying its foreign policy has not changed. U.S.
Sovietologists continue to act like paleontologists, as the editor of
the *World Policy Journal* put it: "They collect a few helpful bones of
evidence and from them claim that they understand the Soviet Union.
But even those with the greatest erudition will, if pressed, concede
how little they really know" (Maines 1987: 93).

The purpose of this study is not to duplicate the voluminous
Western analyses of Gorbachev's new foreign policy assembled by
Western Sovietologists using the traditional methods. Instead our
goal has been the investigation of an additional angle from which
to view Soviet foreign policy. We attempt a brief conspectus of the
utilitarian aspects of the study of "new thinking" as thinking, offering
it as an additional bone to the paleontological/Sovietological ossuary.
The understanding of Soviet "new thinking" as a theoretically viable
Marxist state ideology, we shall argue, enables identification of a
skein of logic in Soviet foreign policy—a pattern that both comple-
ments and corrects the traditional interpretations. The perceived inconsistencies in Soviet behavior—indeed the myth and mystery that
shroud the Gorbachev effect—do not indicate the "prevailing [Soviet]
ideological confusion" (Shenfield 1987: 80) so much as they reveal
our own. We begin with a brief overview of Western analyses of
Soviet foreign policy behavior to show that there is nothing that does
not conform with the pattern in Soviet policy to which we maintain
"new thinking" provides the key.

Western Assessments of Soviet "New Foreign Policy"

As with "new thinking" itself, Western analyses of Soviet foreign policy in the era of "new thinking" have presented themselves in the form of waves (see ch. 1 above, p. 39). In the first wave, attention focussed on the emergence of a new team engaged in the formulation and implementation of foreign policy. Articles from that period tended to equate "new thinking" with the new team. The turnover in foreign policy personnel has been very thorough, with the restructuring of the Foreign Ministry still in progress. In addition to their relative youthfulness, many of the new team members have had experience in the West as diplomats, or have been educated there,* and commentators emphasize that foreign policy has become more innovative, lively, more purposive, and undeniably more intelligent.

Soon after Gorbachev's ascent to power, the West found that the conduct of foreign policy and diplomacy of his new team contrasted sharply with the style of his aging predecessors, which had been characterized by rigidity, confrontationalism, orthodoxy, and so on. "New thinking" was then taken to mean Gorbachev's foreign policy, with the old thinking and old foreign policy of Gorbachev's predecessors assumed as antonymous. There then developed a tendency, particularly on the part of American commentators, to refer to Gorbachev's new foreign policy in glowing terms—as "innovative," "tending to moderation," based on "pragmatism" and "avoidance of confrontation," showing "readiness to compromise" and "flexibility," and the like. Soviet writers have never rejected any of the terms of comparison between old and new and indeed have helped them along: they frequently refer to the Brest-Litovsk peace

*For discussion of the changes in the establishment's top echelon engaged in foreign policy formulation and implementation see footnote above (p. 33) and Appendix 4. The civilian influence in military areas has been strengthened, the diplomatic corps rejuvenated. In addition to the very thorough (and at the time of writing, still continuing) shakeup of the Foreign Ministry that resulted in the creation of a number of new departments (Arms Control, Humanitarian Issues, Information, and the Pacific Ocean Department), the Foreign Ministry's autonomy was curbed vis-à-vis party bodies. One third of ambassadorial positions were replaced in only the first fourteen months of Gorbachev's tenure (there are new Soviet ambassadorial appointments to the United States, China, Japan, Great Britain, France, West Germany, etc.). Diplomatic services have also been extended to areas with no previous diplomatic representation (the South Pacific, for example).

agreement concluded by Lenin as one of many instances of Leninist flexibility from which the new foreign policymakers are believed to draw inspiration.

The Perception of Continuity and Change

Only when the Western study of domestic aspects of Gorbachev's reform was well under way did the second wave of Sovietological analyses begin to address the more substantive parts of the new Soviet foreign policy in terms of specific issues or areas of application. It was soon noticed that in its worldwide activities the new policy was applied unevenly, and many Western commentators noted in surprise the apparent inconsistencies in a new Soviet foreign policy that has in many areas remained rather old in approach.

There has obviously been some continuity even in areas that experienced substantial change (and vice versa), but the commentators would seem to agree that the greatest change occurred in the following groups of issues or areas:

Changed:

Projected image of the Soviet Union;

Withdrawal from Afghanistan and indications of possible withdrawals elsewhere;

Intensified economic and political cooperation with the West, Europe in particular;

Keen interest in economic integration with the West that includes a controlled introduction of elements of capitalism into the Soviet economy;

Higher diplomatic profile in bilateral and multilateral diplomacy on the platform of international organizations, the United Nations in particular, and especially in the field of arms control and disarmament diplomacy and initiatives;

Keen interest in cultural and academic contacts with the West;

More "openness" in selected issues of foreign policy—for example, in regard to disclosing economic and military information traditionally classified secret;

Moves toward rapprochement with the People's Republic of China and special stress on relations with India;

Stress on the Asia-Pacific region, with greatly expanded diplomacy in the region;

Completely new foreign policy establishment, think tank, and diplomatic team.

Thus Western observers have found that positive changes have taken place in Europe and in salient parts of the Third World. They have been much taken by Gorbachev's attitude toward Europe, which he refers to as "our common home," and his readiness to establish friendly relationships with a range of West European leaders, which in the United States is sometimes seen as innovative, moderate, and new. His references to a European "common home" (perhaps by accident inferring the exclusion of Americans), rather than heralding the advent of a new "supraclass" thinking to bridge Europe's two political blocs, seems to some to introduce a new, more purposeful gambit in traditional anti-Americanism—an aspect of Soviet foreign policy that by and large has remained unchanged.

Some observers have commented on the relatively light emphasis placed by Gorbachev on Soviet relations with the Third World. Already by the time of his address to the 27th Party Congress, this omission had become a matter for serious debate. The stress placed by Brezhnev, for example, on national liberation movements has dwindled, and friendly relations with Third World countries that have "liberated themselves but do not follow a socialist path" have been promoted more enthusiastically than relations with those following that path (India and the Association of South East Asian Nations—as against Ethiopia and Mozambique, for example).

Among developments that until quite recently would have been inconceivable, there is the normalization of Sino-Soviet state-to-state and party-to-party relations. The Soviet Union has shown a readiness to compromise on all three of the so-called "three obstacles" to the normalization of relations between the two countries (the disputed border areas and withdrawal of troops from Mongolia, withdrawal from Afghanistan, and a solution of the problem of Kampuchea). Both parties reject the old Stalinist-type Sino-Soviet relations of the 1950s and envisage a new type of relation. Acceleration of the ideological convergence is steady and pronounced: the Soviet concept of peaceful coexistence in its revised form (see p. 71 above) bears close resemblance to the Chinese notion of peaceful coexistence, and Deng's proposal in December 1988 for a New International Political Order coincides in significant areas with Soviet "new thinking."*

Other aspects of the new diplomacy that have interested Western analysts have been the number of proposals issuing from Moscow in the field of arms control and disarmament,† and the chain of proposals to bring about the establishment of nuclear-free zones.

*Cf. Shevardnadze in "E. A. Shevardnadze's Meeting with Deng Xiaoping," 5 February 1989 (reprinted in FBIS-SOV-89-023, 6 February 1989). According to Deng, the New International Political Order presupposes "global unity," strengthening of the United Nations, and is "based on transition from confrontation to dialogue, from tension to detente, and from hegemonism, discrimination, and inequality to peaceful coexistence of all states of the world" (quoted in WEN WEI PO, Hong Kong, FBIS-CHI-89-022).

†In his first two years as Soviet leader, Gorbachev by one count made more than twenty-five distinct arms control moves, most of which were not matched by the Reagan administration (J. Dean, "Gorbachev's Arms Control Moves," *Bulletin of Concerned Scientists* 43, 5 [June 1987]: 34; cited by Sanakoyev 1988: 79). According to a Soviet source, the main Soviet initiatives as of January 1988 included the following:

1. Proposal for a stage-by-stage elimination of nuclear arms under strict international control by the year 2000;
2. Integrated program for creating a comprehensive system of international security, covering military, political, economic, humanitarian, and ecological spheres;
3. Package of detailed and balanced proposals advanced by the USSR at the talks with the U.S. on nuclear and space weapons;
4. Proposal for the complete elimination of chemical weapons under appropriate control and verification measures;
5. Program for reducing the conventional armaments and armed forces in Europe proposed by the USSR jointly with the other Warsaw Treaty states;
6. Package proposals of the Berlin meeting of the Political Consultative Committee (May 1987) set forth in the propositions on the military doctrine of the Warsaw Treaty states;
7. Proposals on medium-range missiles in Europe and on shorter-range missiles;
8. Proposals for ending nuclear test explosions under strict international verification (to achieve greater progress in this direction, the Soviet Union extended its unilateral moratorium on nuclear explosions four times);
9. Proposed broad program for ensuring peace and cooperation in the Asia and Pacific region;
10. Strengthening the UN's prestige and advocating more extensive use of the powers with which the world community has invested that organization and its agencies;
11. Series of proposals on solving regional conflicts ("Seven Decades" 1988: 10).

Although the disarmament proposals and concept of nuclear-free zones derive from the pre-Gorbachev era, the Gorbachev team has lent them powerful impetus. At least eight nuclear-free zones (in Asia, South Africa, Korea, Africa, the Balkans, Latin America, Nordic Europe, and the South Atlantic) have been proposed, together with zones of peace and cooperation (in the South Atlantic, Indian Ocean, and Mediterranean) and a new form called "zone of trust." The upsurge in diplomatic/foreign policy activity has also manifested itself in Gorbachev's proposals for setting up a number of international conferences (on the Middle East, on the Asia-Pacific region, and on the international economic security system). These are consistent with his new emphasis on international law, international organizations (the UN in particular), and diplomacy (multi- or bilateral), but all the areas mentioned have been anticipated in previous Soviet foreign policy.

It is interesting that in response to almost every step of the Soviets' new foreign policy, Western interpreters are disposed to impute altruistic motives to the Soviets. Thus, for example, instead of seeing the Soviet withdrawal from Afghanistan as delivery from a decade of war, it seems to be perceived as yet another triumph of glasnost, flexibility, readiness to compromise, etc.

The foreign policies seen as *unchanged* (or in which change occurs at a much slower rate) and/or which remain in significant regards ambiguous affect three main areas: anti-Americanism, Soviet strategic doctrine, and Soviet relations with its satellites—in Eastern Europe in particular.

First, the unchanged anti-Americanism and unremitting hostility toward the United States, particularly toward the U.S. "military-industrial complex," is in sharp contrast with the extension of new friendly relations worldwide.

Second, the changes in Soviet strategic doctrine remain ambiguous and allow a multitude of interpretations concerning Soviet strategic goals and objectives (Peterson and Trulock 1988; Holloway 1988/89). Western analysts are seriously divided in their evaluation of the thinking that underlies the sudden array of arms control and disarmament initiatives, including the steps taken in Soviet "unilateral disarmament" in conventional weaponry (embarked upon in early 1989). The semantic shift from the earlier "reliable sufficiency" to the current "reasonable sufficiency" is also highly ambiguous. It sheds little light on what is to be regarded as "sufficient"—and for what purpose. In other words, the Soviet goal of military parity and maintenance of an offensive capability could be unaffected. By contrast, the serious difficulties experienced in keeping up with the United States in the technological aspects of the arms race are a known factor, and in light of the gravity of the issues involved, it has to be considered that such proposals as a freeze at present levels of weaponry to staunch the economic drain of armsbuilding, and so forth, could be made for reasons other than humanitarian—that the new strategic doctrine and its attendant "high profile" arms control initiatives are designed to slow the arms race and in so doing hamper American development of sophisticated defensive weapons systems (Wettig 1987b, 1987c, 1988b, 1988c; Griffith 1986; Lizichev 1987; Gareyev 1987).

In the opinion of some commentators, the key to the new strategic doctrine (as contained in "new thinking") is the rather old emphasis on the political nature of national security. By declaring security exclusively a matter of political concern, military considerations are subordinated even more than in the past to political concerns, which has the effect of depriving them of their autonomy. As it turns out, it is only through its political referents that the new military doctrine can be defined as defensive. The argument here runs very much along old-fashioned lines: since the Soviet Union is socialist and thus peace-loving, it cannot be aggressive. On the other hand, Western imperialism (now referred to as neo-globalism) is inherently offensive. At present, the defensive nature of Soviet political-military goals is further deduced from the general principles of "new thinking," specifically from the eagerness of the Soviets to prevent war between East and West, and from their willingness to take under their defensive umbrella the entire socialist community (where earlier it protected only the USSR). The Soviets insist that the rationale of the new doctrine of "defensive defense" is no more than the defense of the USSR against imperialist aggression should war break out. This argument is contradicted by repeated exhortations by Soviet military theoreticians that the USSR must strengthen its military capability and maintain a high level of military preparedness. Since the definitions of what is and is not defensive or offensive derive from exclusively political considerations of who (applying the Marxist terms of reference) is involved, it means that Soviet military strategy, in contrast to the implied promise of "new thinking," continues a policy of not excluding offensive military operations while at the same time resolutely promoting a defensive image.

The fragility of these arguments suggests that it may be too soon to rush to the conclusion that the new Soviet concept of national security is no longer conceived in zero-sum terms (Light 1988: 310). The fact that the concept of international or global security is so argued is another matter.

Third, despite proposals to withdraw some divisions from Eastern Europe, the Soviet relation to its East European satellites remains unchanged insofar as there is no suggestion that the East European countries can exercise their right of self-determination and, if they so wish, leave the Soviet bloc. Various proposals for changes to multiparty political systems in some East European countries must be implemented before the Soviet attitude on this issue can be clarified.

Soviet attempts to introduce perestroika and glasnost into Eastern Europe (leaving the form they are to take up to the individual countries) have left the region in unprecedented turmoil—no doubt exacerbated by the fact that Eastern Europe is the last area to be theoretically rationalized in terms of "new thinking." Commentators note that the shortest, most perfunctory chapter in Gorbachev's *Perestroika* deals with Eastern Europe. In it he refers to the sovereign rights of parties, implying that the party structure is not subject to perestroika. Gorbachev's own attitude toward Eastern Europe seems ambivalent. On the one hand, he is eager to tackle the East European issue and project a more accommodating Soviet image, but on the other hand he ignores all opportunities, including visits to all socialist countries in 1987, to reformulate the Brezhnev doctrine of socialist internationalism. Even though many high-ranking Soviet officials have declared that the Brezhnev doctrine has been "left behind," the doctrine of socialist internationalism has been endorsed in all major political documents adopted since 1985.* Gorbachev is prepared to acknowledge "deformations and mistakes linked with the earlier

---

*Such as in the program of the CPSU, in the protocols extending the life of the Warsaw Pact, apropos the adoption of a new "comprehensive program for COMECON to the year 2000," and in Gorbachev's speech to the seventieth anniversary of the October Revolution.

period of the history of socialism," and talks about the "unconditional independence" of socialist countries (1989: 68), but the parameters of Soviet tolerance remain unclear (see Dawisha and Valdez 1987; Gati 1988/89). It is noteworthy that economic and military aid to "satellites" in the Third World has continued undiminished.

Rationales

There are many possible explanations why some areas of Soviet foreign policy have changed and others have not, and why the Soviet Union feels a need to maintain a high profile in certain areas and not in others. They seem to revolve mainly around the notion of Soviet weakness. Until the final consolidation in power of Gorbachev and his team (by November 1988), we heard a great deal about Gorbachev's own weakness in leadership (against internal opposition in the Politburo from the left and the right, from the bureaucracy, and from general inertia). The discussion of the weakness and insecurities of the USSR, whether domestic, political, ethnic, economic, or geopolitical, still continues.

Soviet foreign policy, then, is seen as devised to counter the weakness and reverse the processes of decline. It is argued by some that in order to remain at the helm Gorbachev needs to conduct his foreign policy so as to score points against his domestic opposition. Alternatively it is said that Gorbachev's purpose is to create a suitable international environment for advancing the perestroika of Soviet society. Other explanations are that Gorbachev's foreign policy is designed to salvage the world status of the USSR—either as one of the two superpowers or, more modestly, as one of several great powers in the envisaged evolution of a multipolar world. Many Western interpreters see Gorbachev as a closet social democrat (why else would he draw so much on the ideas of Willy Brandt and Olaf Palme?); others see him as trying to halt the process of economic and political marginalization that pushes the Soviet Union ever further toward the status of a Third World country; others postulate that the "disintegration of the Soviet Empire" is at stake with reports of continuing economic difficulties and ethnic disturbances at home and within its East European satellites.

The most recent wave in the West's response to the Gorbachev effect brings with it the heady conclusion that the West has won (or almost won) the Cold War, assuming the decline of the USSR as the other superpower. Gorbachev meanwhile continues to tread the stage of a suddenly narrowed world, and although his speeches are more appropriate to a victor, he is taken to Western hearts with an eager embrace. The international diplomatic triumphs manifest in, for example, the address by a "vanquished" Gorbachev to the United Nations in December 1988 have not been found to contradict in any way the optimistic view of his foreign policy as an unprecedented

> example of a great imperial power deliberately contracting its empire by so much within a year. The downfall of the Roman Empire took place from outside forces over a period of nearly 1,000 years. The British Empire was dissolved gradually over a period of some 40 years. . . . The change in behavior on the ground has reflected a change in attitude toward the outside world. . . . [Mikhail Gorbachev] . . . visited Washington as though he and Ronald Reagan were fellow members of the club of heads of government, no longer emissaries from hostile camps parlaying under a flag of truce. In 1988, the Soviet Union abandoned its isolationism born in the Stalin era and sought to become, and in many ways actually did, a member of the family of nations. . . . It is not so much that the cold war is over. It is rather that the conditions that bred it have given way to new conditions in which the "superpowers" are ceasing to be super powers.*

Perceptions of Soviet Weakness and "Soviet Threat"

Gorbachev's perestroika acknowledges a domestic crisis of the Soviet system—a Soviet weakness "publicly aired" in line with glasnost. The dismantling of the image of Soviet threat is the immediate goal of Soviet "new thinking" and a prerequisite of its success. The combination of perestroika, glasnost, and "new thinking" has produced near total Western acceptance of the idea of Soviet weakness and, more important, has led to reconsideration of the nature and potency of the Soviet threat. Thus "new thinking" has already—

*Joseph C. Harsch, "The Year the Soviets Came from the Cold—into the 'Family of Nations,'" Christian Science Monitor, 23 December 1988, pp. 7, 9.

within a remarkably short period of time—played a substantial part in effecting a major shift in Western thinking about the USSR. In other words, an attitude that before Gorbachev had characterized only Western Marxist or radical liberal groups has now become the prevailing Western perspective. In the 1950s and 1960s a small group of U.S. revisionist historians, influenced by the New Left, assigned chief responsibility to the United States for the Cold War, and particularly for the fabrication of the notion of a Soviet threat. A generation later, in the late 1970s and early 1980s, the Western Marxist theorists of what they called the "New Cold War" used the alleged inability of the USSR to pose a real threat to the West to heap added blame on the United States and further absolve the USSR for its role in the Cold War.*

However, the recent Western preoccupation with select areas of Soviet weakness (how much to help Gorbachev?), in conjunction with possibly declaring the impending end of the Cold War and of the Soviet threat, is based on a different foundation than the revisionist interpretations of the Cold War. To Western (and Soviet) Marxists the Soviet Union is inherently different from capitalist America: with all its weaknesses and deformations, it is a "post-revolutionary" or "post-capitalist" society without the aggressive character of its capitalist-imperialist counterpart. It is also seen as economically, militarily, and politically weak. It is worth remarking that much of non-Marxist reasoning about what attitude should be taken toward Gorbachev's Soviet Union is often based on a less coherent footing. This becomes apparent as soon as the USSR ceases to be perceived as an inherently aggressive power committed to expansionism by its Marxist ideology. Beyond that point, as Charles Gati observes, we do not possess firm evidence on which to base conclusions regarding the relationship between Soviet domestic and foreign policy. In light of the historical record we cannot be sure what the causal relationship is between Soviet domestic economic weakness or strength and Soviet foreign policy. We do not know if a weak or strong USSR will incline (temporarily or permanently) toward a cooperative or confrontational

---

*For a review of this literature, see V. Kubálková and A. A. Cruickshank, "The 'New Cold War' in 'Critical International Relations Studies,'" *Review of International Studies* 12 (1986); see also F. Halliday, *The Making of the Second Cold War* (London: Verso, 1983).

course, any more than we can know conclusively the effect of ideological rigidity or flexibility on Soviet foreign policy behavior.*

While there is evidence enough of Soviet economic weakness,
the status of ideology in the Soviet Union in general (and in foreign
policy in particular) has not so far been seriously addressed in the
West.[†] The crucial question is how much glasnost and what quality
of "new thinking" will be regarded in the West as sufficient for Soviet
writing to be taken seriously as a source of Soviet thinking about
Soviet foreign policy.

In circumstances where only marginal Western attention is directed toward Soviet texts, "new thinking" has been taken to mean
primarily de-ideologization. It is worth repeating that, contrary to
popular belief, the Western thesis of a "de-ideologizing Soviet Union"
as part of "new thinking" is not supported by the Soviets' pronouncement of a need to "de-ideologize international relations." They refer
to different things. Similarly the Western linkage between Soviet
domestic and foreign policy is not confirmed by any comparable
linkage made by Soviet writers. They too mean different things. In
both cases the foreign policy is evaluated as aggressive-conflictual
or cooperative, but the two evaluations are based on different sets
of values. One of the purposes of "new thinking" is the provision
of a new set of all-human, global values which will supplant the
traditional Western values. The apparent agreement by Soviet and
Western writers that the Cold War is over derives in the Soviet case
not from the perception of the end of Soviet ideology but of the end
of Western ideology. Soviet and Western Marxists see the Cold War

---

*Gati points out that no Western analyst has been able to offer evidence of the
validity of any of the following hypotheses:
1. Domestic weakness leads to foreign policy accommodation.
2. Domestic weakness leads to foreign policy assertiveness.
3. Domestic strength leads to foreign policy accommodation.
4. Domestic strength leads to foreign policy assertiveness.
5. A rigid ideological environment leads to foreign policy assertiveness.
6. A decline in ideological fervor leads to foreign policy accommodation.
("The Stalinist Legacy in Soviet Foreign Policy," *The Soviet Union in the 1980s:
Proceedings of the Academy of Political Science* (1984: 218ff.).

[†]Soviet writers (for example, *Izvestiya* commentator Alexander Bovin) complain
that glasnost has not been extended to the sphere of international relations (1988:
6), while Soviet leaders complain that Soviet social scientists are not "thinking
new" on the subject.

as founded on Western "old thinking," fuelled by the contrived image of a Soviet threat, and its demise, according to Soviet writers, is a result of the Soviet adoption of "new thinking." When joined with glasnost and perestroika, "new thinking" exposes the fraudulence of the old thinking and through the establishment of Soviet intellectual ascendancy makes Soviet world leadership credible.

A New Soviet Strategy of Foreign Policy

It might be appropriate at this point to recapitulate some of the main theses of "new thinking" discussed in Chapters 2 and 3 to anticipate the final thesis of this study—namely, that "new thinking" sheds light on some of the obscure or ambiguous aspects of Soviet foreign policy.

To this end we show in graphic form (Table 1) our contention that "new thinking" was conceived as the antithesis of Western "old thinking"—countervailing in all important respects (even terminologically) the perceived world hegemony of the United States. (We use hegemony and counter-hegemony in the Gramscian sense.) In this regard "new thinking" is an important index of the reorientation of Soviet foreign policy.

Our sketch of the counter-hegemonic model of Soviet strategy (Table 2) represents a progression from the summary in terms of a new rationale, revised target areas, and methods for the achievement of newly identified short-term objectives and regional priorities of Soviet foreign policy. On the Soviets' own admission, the main thrust of "new thinking" as the "counter-hegemony" is a new tactical orientation that derives from evaluation of their own weakness vis-à-vis capitalist strength. It deals with new means for the achievement of essentially unchanged ends—namely, the historically preordained replacement of capitalism by socialism—a theme invariably returned to by every Soviet author. The areas of change and continuity in Soviet foreign policy as perceived by Sovietologists (see above, pp. 93–99) can be regrouped as shown in Table 2.

Table 1

Soviet Analysis of the U.S. Hegemony and the Philosophy of Counter-Hegemony

	U.S. HEGEMONY is based on:	USSR (Gramscian) COUNTER-HEGEMONY to be based on:
Political system	The states-system described in old thinking (power realism) as consisting of global anarchy—i.e. the absence of global values and the absence of effective international organization with the relations of sovereign and armed states regulated by the mechanism of balance of power and its variations (such as nuclear deterrence)	An international (world) society described in "new thinking" as predicated on global values (the interdependence of survival in the nuclear age), strengthening of international organizations (the UN, ICJ, etc.) and of the mechanism of balance of interests of states that enjoy autonomy ("freedom of choice") but renounce the use of force and are disarming
Economic system	The interdependent capitalist world economy led by the neo-globalist USA	The cooperative (interdependent) relation of socialist market economies with the much stronger capitalist economies
Ideology	The old thinking of the Cold War with the alleged threat of the non-democratic USSR and its expansionist totalitarian Marxist-Leninist ideology of world communism	New Thinking of the end of the Cold War ("de-ideologization of international relations") and of the end of the states-system discrediting the notion of Soviet threat—viz., Soviet domestic reform (perestroika, glasnost), arms control initiatives and apparent reversal of expansionism The intellectual and moral ascendancy of the USSR and world socialism over morally and politically corrupt capitalism

Table 2

Counter-Hegemonic Foreign Policy Strategy

1. It is a strategy of weakness for the achievement of unmodified Marxist goals.

2. The targets are (Gramscian) civil societies: the Western populaces and world society.

3. The economical method consists of intellectualized foreign policy based simultaneously on:

   A. Dissemination and manipulation of ideas and of the world's global consciousness with the help of the historic bloc ("new thinking");

   B. The coercive military mechanism relegated to a backup role.

4. Immediate, simultaneously pursued objectives:

   A. To break the U.S. hegemony;

   B. To influence a new ideo-political global consensus (restructure international organization and international law);

   C. To forge integrative links with an interdependent world economy so as to anchor economically the counter-hegemonic Soviet bloc.

5. Changed regional priorities to reflect the above: worldwide weaning of U.S. allies and other forms of "denial" (nuclear-free zones, ambiguous arms control proposals to weaken the Western alliance) as alternative to advance by overt military expansionism.

In elaboration of Table 2:

1. Soviet "new thinking" is the starting point of a strategy of weakness contrived in the face of the failure of the Soviet economic and ideological model and Soviet inability to maintain its geopolitical gains throughout the world without the use of military force. Military methods have become too costly in both financial and public opinion terms. The Soviets will continue to espouse modernized Marxist doctrine and to prescribe long-term Marxist goals that include creation of a changed socioeconomic world order based on a different ideo-political consensus. The main reason for the lack of success in countering U.S. hegemony in recent years has been the hold of "old thinking" on the world's consciousness, together with a neo-globalist U.S. foreign policy. Soviet counter-hegemony is designed to break that U.S. hegemony in every conceivable way.

2. The primary targets of Soviet foreign policy attention are two types of "civil societies": the civil societies of Western countries and the international civil society that is evolving around international organizations and international law. To the Western civil societies the USSR presents itself as the custodian of all-human and global values; to the international civil society it seeks to establish, by way of a stream of proposals and initiatives, the seniority and ascendancy required for the translation of these initiatives into the planned perestroika of the international order.*

3. The preferred methods include the use of political and propaganda instruments, intellectual contacts and exchanges, and a high diplomatic profile that projects an innovative, flexible, and altruistic image. These are paralleled by initiatives in the areas of international law and international organizations, particularly in the field of arms control. Most crucial here is the fashioning of a new image of the USSR dissociated from the Soviet threat to be achieved domestically by displays of benevolence through implementation of glasnost policies, fair treatment of dissidents, and a more liberal approach to human rights, and internationally through the advocacy of popular causes in international forums.

The emphasis is on the formation and dissemination of ideas and the creation of an intellectual ascendancy: hence references to an "intellectualized" foreign policy. The ability to allude to a body of ideas that are both acceptable to Western audiences and compatible with Marxist historical materialism is of critical importance (cf. the first nine points of "new thinking," p. 6 above).

The high diplomatic profile of a self-appointed intellectual leader of the world society and guardian of the all-human, global values contrasts with a low-profile use of military power, coercive pressures, and maintenance of a deterrent capability. The changing Soviet military posture is consistent with Gramscian ideas which make a great deal of sense when seen as the pivotal ideas of "new thinking." Evaluation of unilateral disarmament, arms control

*In addition to determining the *shape* of global things to come, the Gorbachev regime has been determining the *pace*. Gorbachev himself often dictates the agenda, bombarding his counterparts with a series of options, offering initiatives in rapid sequence, and addressing issues on several fronts at the same time. The importance of the propaganda aspect of "new thinking" has been most apparent in the area of arms control diplomacy.

measures, and the Soviet defensive defense are made difficult by the numerical intricacies of the strategic equation, but there can be little doubt that the role of the military machine is being shifted to the background—a position it is likely to occupy so long as foreign policy objectives can be achieved by less aggravating methods. The "new thinkers" appear to have concluded that, given the ready availability of nuclear and conventional military power as deterrent, the new rules of international politics set forth in "new thinking" are guarantee enough of foreign policy success, provided the West will agree to play by these rules.

4. The strategy has three interrelated immediate objectives that are difficult to separate but which will produce a strong Soviet Union, an intellectual world leader, and a pioneer in the restructuring of the existing world order:

First, to break the neo-globalist U.S. international hegemony by an explicitly anti-American course of isolating and weakening the United States through the piecemeal erosion of its military alliances and blocs, the tarnishing of its international image, and the discrediting of the notion of Soviet threat. With the consequent crumbling of the Western alliance, even the most stubborn of U.S. allies may experience a change of heart.

Second, to counter the old thinking and establish a new ideo-political global consensus by achieving intellectual leadership within a new, globally composed historical bloc of intellectuals, opinion makers, and world leaders.

Third, by way of bridges into Western societies, to bring about economic and technological integration with the capitalist countries and thereby forge the economic strength that is a prerequisite for the solid establishment of the counter-hegemonic bloc. Recent successes and eager competition by Western financiers to render assistance need no documentation.

5. The new pattern is reflected in changed regional priorities that are focussed first on the United States and its Western allies, in Europe and elsewhere. In the Third World the stress is on the cost-effectiveness of any foreign policy engagement. Third World geopolitical gains will not be surrendered unless matched by commensurate diplomatic gains elsewhere, but other conversions to the socialist model in the traditional Soviet style will not be sought. Economic

integration of the Third World with the capitalist countries will be encouraged. Recent advances in the Third World highlight the Asia-Pacific region as particularly suitable for testing the cost-effectiveness of the counter-hegemonic strategy.*

*The new reach of the Soviets into hitherto untouched areas was foreshadowed in Gromyko's adage from the 1970s that there is no decision taken, no area existing in which the USSR has no interest. In his important speech in Vladivostok in August 1986, Gorbachev declared the Asia-Pacific region to be something of a Soviet backyard. There duly followed the opening of diplomatic relations in these new areas, an increase in visits by senior Soviet officials, and the operations of the Soviet fishing fleet have been extended upon the discovery of fish around the South Pacific islands (including around New Zealand and Australia)—areas now become nuclear free.

Chapter 6

"NEW THINKING" AS A CHALLENGE TO
WESTERN "OLD THINKING"

Our argument in this study is based on the proposition that
three areas that have traditionally received little or no attention in
the United States are crucial for understanding Gorbachev's "new
thinking" on international relations. First, Soviet writing, emanating
as it does from a non-democratic society, has not been regarded as
a source of Soviet thinking or as having any significant impact on
Soviet foreign policy; second, legalist-moralist approaches to international politics have traditionally been dismissed as utopian and
idealist in favor of the power realist calculus; and third, Marxism as
a philosophical tradition has been ignored, misunderstood, or dismissed as unimportant.

It is beyond the scope of this study to analyze these Western
blindspots, but it is within them that Gorbachev's "new thinking"
has been developing. As its name suggests, "new thinking" is *thinking*; its prima facie expression is a moralist-legalist approach to international politics that rejects power realism and stresses issues of
ethics, international law, and international organizations as the main
tools for the restructuring of the states-system. Finally, with all of
Gorbachev's contrived un-Marxian lexicon, his legalistic moralism,
and his bewildering screen of "orderly" diplomatic activity, the home-
coming gift of the prodigal returned to his "family of nations" is a
new form of Marxism: the Soviet leader describes himself as a Marxist.

The failure to engage in more serious scrutiny has been insti-
tutionalized in the now somewhat hidebound disciplinary limitations
of the Western social sciences. Through the cracks and fissures, the
Soviet concept of "new thinking" has slipped without notice, or at
any rate has managed to evade a firm grasp. One reason for this is

not difficult to find: the Sovietologist and the theorist of international relations do not follow closely the concerns of the other, and it is unusual for either to know Marxism. Yet Soviet "new thinking" clearly requires a perspective that combines the knowledge of all three. Without that perspective, the subject matter is too theoretical for the Sovietologists, who often begin in empiricism and end there in a historical scan of puzzling Soviet behavior, seeking to discover if there is anything that deserves to be called "new." Their approach contrasts with that of Western philosophers, Western Marxists, and Western international relations theorists, who study neither old nor new Soviet thinking because it does not fit any of their standards of what constitutes thinking, or philosophy, or Marxism, or, for that matter, international relations theory.

As a consequence, the range of interpretations of "new thinking" has become skewed. Those who regard the Soviet advance in the West with concern and apprehension are in the process of being deprived of arguments by the intellectual "gatekeepers" whose attention tends now to be turned to events within their own communities. In the continuing change in the Western intellectual climate, new taboos are developing. The attitudes of the Cold War are in many ways in the process of being reversed, and those who warrant the Soviet designation of thinking "old" become not infrequently the objects of the Western gatekeepers' search.

The approach we adopt is not one commonly applied to "new thinking" in the West, but the methodology is certainly not uncommon in Western studies of the history of ideas, of theory of international relations, or of political philosophy. We see no reason why a Soviet intellectual/ideological product that calls itself "New Thinking," "New Political Thinking," or indeed "New Philosophy of International Relations" should be exempted from as critical a scholarly scrutiny as would certainly be applied to any Western intellectual products. Yet even now, when many in the West purportedly are of the opinion that glasnost has provided the hitherto missing ingredient and leaven of academic freedom in Soviet society,* the same academics busy themselves with analyzing each other's theories and

---

*Already the "critical" international relations theorists have begun to sensitize mainstream international relations students to the fact that the exclusion of Soviet writing on the grounds of its being ideological is no longer justified. The newly emerged left wing of the Anglo-American theorists of international relations, in

ignore the writings of Shakhnazarov, Bovin, Plimak, Kortunov, Primakov, or other intellectual counsellors of Gorbachev.

Hence we began with an analysis of Soviet texts dealing with "new thinking," rather than setting these aside and imputing to the Soviets what they "must be thinking" as deduced from their foreign policy behavior, using Soviet quotations to confirm our own thinking. We have assembled associations which invariably crop up in Soviet writing under the rubric "New Thinking" (chapter 1). Through examination of the circumstances of the concept's enunciation and development, we find persuasive evidence that the term *new thinking* was chosen neither to indicate the Gorbachev team's wish to dissociate themselves from their Marxist predecessors nor to give up Marxism as the foundation of the Soviet state ideology (chapter 2). "New thinking" is neither Gorbachev's brainchild nor a product of glasnost—by which we mean the outcome of free debate among foreign policy specialists. Nor is "new thinking" a set of ideas hastily put together to help redress a serious domestic crisis. It is, as Gorbachev said to the UN Secretary-General, "not the fruit of improvisation or facile arguments; it is profoundly considered and nurtured" (*Pravda*, 9 December 1988). With that discovery, the ten associations of "new thinking" we found turn out to be merely the tip of the iceberg—a small part of a profoundly significant and far-reaching intellectual/ideological change and reorientation of Soviet foreign policy.

We refer to the broad Western (as well as the Soviet) tradition of Marxist thought to show that the associations of "new thinking" are not incompatible with Marxist precepts, and that the philosophical

---

a spirited attack on the reigning realist paradigm, have opened the door to those who would study Soviet "new thinking" as a theory of international relations. Most critical writers argue that all processes of cognition have to be seen within a social context—an argument that goes back to Marx and Mannheim. As R. W. Cox puts it, it means that "theory is always for someone and for some purpose. All theories have a perspective . . . which derives from specific social and political time and space. . . . There is accordingly no such thing as theory in itself, divorced from a standpoint in time and space. When any theory so represents itself, it is more important to examine it as an ideology, and to lay bare its concealed perspective" ("Social Factors, States and World Orders," pp. 129–30). It would seem to follow that if knowledge is always socially and ideologically bound, then the continuing dismissal of Soviet "new thinking" is illogical. Soviet thinking is unashamedly ideological, and its manipulative uses are undisguised.

framework within which the new Soviet state ideology is cast is Marxist (chapter 3). Western Marxists have always found Soviet Marxist-Leninist thinking of the Stalin/Brezhnev variety to be un-Marxist, or a Marxist aberration. Thus, with the Western Marxists as guides, we examine "new thinking" as a possible renaissance of Marxism. In the Western variants of Marxism (or post-Marxism), there is very little of orthodox class and economic determinism. One of the effects of "new thinking," therefore, is to bring the Soviet variant closer to its estranged Western cousins.

The ten associations of "new thinking" do not suggest a revision but merely a postponement of traditional Marxist ends: more immediate objectives are set, and new means of achieving these ends are sought. It is only when "new thinking" is understood as a search for new tactics that its true novelty can be appreciated. It is in this regard that both the new Soviet theory of international relations that evolves out of "new thinking" (chapter 4) as well as the new foreign policy (chapter 5) make sense. Otherwise we are left nonplussed, with the notion of the miraculous transformation of Gorbachev's USSR disarming unilaterally and dismantling its dominions before our eyes. Some Western observers believe Gorbachev is willing and capable of such a *tour de force*, defying in the process both the historical record and the "natural laws" of international politics.

After his address to the UN General Assembly in December 1988, many Western commentators were brought belatedly to the realization that Gorbachev has in mind a coup of a different sort, and that he is engaged in an attempt to bring perestroika not only to Soviet society but to the world order as well. Historical parallels between Gorbachev and Woodrow Wilson, Olaf Palme, and Willy Brandt suggest themselves, but Gorbachev is a Marxist whose obvious predecessor is the "Grotian Marxist" Antonio Gramsci. With Gramsci in mind, "new thinking" and the extraordinary array of Gorbachev initiatives begin at last to fall into place. We draw attention to Gramsci's strategy of counter-hegemony not to suggest that Gramsci's *Prisoner's Notebooks* are a blueprint of "new thinking," but to show that within Marxist tradition (starting with Marx himself!) it is possible to shift from class struggle and coercive methods to culture and consciousness, to the molding of consensus along the lines set by a "historical bloc" of intellectuals. According to Soviet writers, the new transnational historical bloc has already been at work, and the consummation of their collective efforts is the globally shared "new thinking." Gorbachev's repeated references to "world society" may be seen as corresponding to an extended Gramscian civil society, which in Gorbachev's "new thinking" replaces the states-system. Again in Gramscian terms, Gorbachev's shift is from a "war of maneuver" to a "war of position"—the former based on invasion and occupation, the latter much less profligate of material and good-will. The latter strategy depends on invitations by target societies into their "homes"—the notion of "our home" conveying to Gorbachev not only "our planetary home," but "our European home," "our Asia-Pacific home," and, in the case of the United Nations, "our house of peace."*

Just as it proved for the Italian Communist Party in the 1930s, a Gramscian model appears to be the only sensible option for the Soviet Union in the present circumstances. It is the only way that a weak and weakening superpower with nothing but military muscle to support its geopolitical gains can go. The Gramscian theory opens up a dimension of conflict and confrontation beyond the power realist use of threat of force, or beyond the standard Western understanding of propaganda.

Gramsci's strategy, it might be argued, did not work, but then again it was never put to the test—except for a brief episode of abortive Eurocommunism centered around the Communist parties of France and Italy, from whence Gramscian ideas moved to the Soviet Union (Berner and Dahm 1987). Gramsci developed his theories in a Fascist jail without the benefit of Marxist think tanks or the research institutes of a modern Marxist superpower: a super-power which, in line with the central Marxist notion of unity of theory and practice, seems to be hazarding all its hopes and future (Gorbachev's words) on making a theoretical breakthrough.

The new strategy may not work for the Soviet Union either, nor yield its counter-hegemonic goals and aspirations. Our contention is, however, that in the meantime, and before another Soviet Congress

*In this context an argument we advanced some time before the adoption of "new thinking" by the USSR seems germane: "[F]ollowing Gramsci's [prescient] counsel in regard to the war of manoeuvre and 'counter-hegemony' . . . [t]he only agency capable of restructuring the states-system would indeed then appear to be the Machiavellian Centaur, a mix of coercion and consent, of authority and hegemony, violence and civilization" (Kubálková and Cruickshank 1985 and 1989: 203–4).

enunciates a newer strategy, a Western understanding of the counter-hegemonic pattern can shed light on current Soviet practice. If additionally it helps provide an interpretative framework for anticipating and analyzing future initiatives, we might be spared further surprises.

In our view "new thinking" is an attempt by the Soviet superpower to find a Marxist foreign policy foundation that is not only significantly different from that of the United States, but also will allow the socio-economically weaker USSR to establish the rules and set the pace in the next phase of the "historical struggle." Judging from the powerful push it has already given to the "historical process," it may be time for our own thinking to reassess Soviet weakness and take account of our own.

APPENDIXES

Appendix 1

SELECTED BIBLIOGRAPHY OF
SOVIET SOURCES ON "NEW THINKING"

"A Real Step towards a Safe World." 1988. *International Affairs*, February.

"Armiia revolucii, armiia naroda" [The army of revolution, the army of the people]. 1988. *Kommunist* 3.

Adamovich, Ales. 1988. "Problems with the New Way of Thinking." In Gromyko and Hellman, eds.

Afanaseev, V. 1986. "O novom politicheskom myshlenii" [On new political thinking]. *Pravda*, 5 December.

Afanasyevky, N.; Tarasinkevich, E.; Shvedov, A. 1988. "Between Yesterday and Today." *International Affairs* 5.

Aganbegyan, A., ed. 1988. *Perestroika Annual.* London: Futura Publications.

Agayev, E., and Kozyrev, A. 1988. "The United Nations and Reality." *International Affairs* 5 (April).

Akhtamzyan, A., and Kapchenko, N. 1988. "Turning Point." *International Affairs* 4 (April).

Antipov, A. 1988. "Paguosh-88" [Pugwash-88]. *Kommunist* 14 (September).

Antonovich, I. 1988. "Dialectics of an Integral World." *International Affairs* 3.

Arab-Ogly, E. A. 1988. "Realities of New Thinking: From Confrontation to Cooperation." *Kommunist* 2 (January); reprinted in JPSR-UKO-88-007, 4 April.

Arbatov, G. 1987. "Militarizm i sovremennoe obshchestvo" [Militarism and contemporary society]. *Kommunist* 2 (January).

————. 1988. "New Political Thinking in the USSR." *Politika* (Belgrade), 23 October; reprinted in FBIS-SOV-88-221, 16 November.

Beglov, S. 1987. "The New Political Thinking and Present-day Realities." *International Affairs*, November.

————. 1988. "Security—Ours and Theirs." *International Affairs* 3.

Bekhtereva, N. P. 1988. "Dangers and Opportunities for Change from a Physiologist's Point of View." In Gromyko and Hellman, eds.

Bogdanov, R. 1984. "From the Balance of Forces to a Balance of Interests." *International Affairs* 4 (April).

Bovin, A. 1986a. *The Imperative of the Nuclear Age.* Moscow: Novosti.

NOTE: Wherever possible we refer to an English translation.

————. 1986b. "Novoe myshlenie—trebovanie iadernogo veka" [New thinking—a requirement of the nuclear age]. *Kommunist* 10.

————. 1987. "Perestroika i sudby socializma "[Perestroika and the destiny of socialism]. *Izvestiya*, 11 July.

————. 1988a "Let's Break the Ice on Foreign Policy." *Moscow News* 24.

————. 1988b. "October and Peaceful Coexistence." *Izvestiya*, 6 November; reprinted in FBIS-SOV-88-217.

————. 1988c. "New Thinking–New Policy." *Kommunist* 9 (June); reprinted in JPRS-UKO-88-015, 6 October.

————. .1988d. "Perestroika i vneshnaya politika" [Restructuring and foreign policy]. *Izvestiya*, June 16.

————. 1988e. "Mirovoe soobshchestvo i mirovoe pravitelstvo: otklik na statiu 'Mirovoe soobshchestvo upravliaemo'" [World society and world government: a reply to the article 'Governability of the World Society'" (Shakhnazarov 1988a)]. *Pravda*, 1 February.

Bromlei, Iulian V. 1986. "Improving National Relations in the USSR." *Kommunist* 8; reprinted in *Soviet Law and Government* 31, 2 (Fall 1987).

Bunkina, M., and Petrov, N. 1986. "Vsemirnoe khozaistvo—ekonomicheskii fundament mirovogo sosushchestvovania" [World economy—the basis of peaceful coexistence]. *MEMO*, September.

Burlatsky, F. M. 1988a. "New Thinking about Socialism." In Gromyko and Hellman, eds.

————. 1988b. *Novoe myshlenie*. Moscow: Politizdat.

Bykov, Vasil. 1985. "On the High Ground of Conscience." *Literaturnaia gazeta*, October 9; reprinted in *Soviet Law and Government* 36, 1 (Summer 1987).

Cagolov, G., and Kireev, A. 1988. "Vremiia yadernykh dospekhov" [A time of nuclear successes]. *Pravda*, 4 January.

Chervov, Nikolai. 1988. "Mighty Factor for World Peace." *International Affairs* 3 (March).

CPSU [Communist Party of the Soviet Union]. 1985. "Programma Kommunisticheskoi Partii Sovetskogo Soyuza: novaya redaktsiya" [Program of the CPSU: new edition]; reprinted in *Kommunist* 4 (1986).

"Delhi Declaration." 1986. *Pravda*, November.

Dobrynin, A. 1986a. "Za bezyadernyi mir, navstrechu XXI veku" [Toward a non-nuclear world for the 21st century]. *Kommunist* 8.

————. 1986b. "Glavnaia sotsialnaia sila sovremennosti" [The main social force at present]. *Kommunist* 16.

————. 1987. "The Vladivostok Programme: Progress and Prospects." *World Marxist Review* 30, 9 (September).

Falin, V. 1988. "Dismantling the Image of the Enemy." *Moscow News* 20.

Fedorov, B. 1988. "The USSR's Foreign Debt: A Need for New Approaches." *Moscow News* 44, 30 (October).

Fedorov, E., and Fedorov, Yu. 1979. "Globalnye problemy sovremennosti i razoruzhenie" [Contemporary global problems and disarmament]. *MEMO* 1.

Fedoseyev, P. N. 1986. "Dialektika v sovremennom mire" [Dialectics in the contemporary world]. *Voprosy filosofii* 5.

————. 1987. "O perestroike raboty v oblasti obshchestvennykh nauk" [On the perestroika of work in social science areas]. *Voprosy filosofii* 5.

Frolov, I. 1986. "Nauchitsa myslit i deistvovat po-novomu" [Learning and behaving in a new way]. *MEMO* 10.

————. 1988. "Man, Science, Humanism." *Kommunist* 11 (July); reprinted in JPRS-UKO-88-017, 27 October.

Fyodorov, V. 1987. "The UN and a Comprehensive International Security System." *International Affairs* 9 (September).

Galkin, A. 1988. "Novoe politicheskoe myshlenie i problemy rabochego dvizhenia" [New political thinking and the problems of the workers' movement]. *MEMO* 5.

Gareyev, M. A. 1985. "The Creative Character of Soviet Military Science in the Great Patriotic War." *Voyenno-istoricheskiy zhurnal* [Military historical journal] 7 (July).

————. 1987. *Sovetskaya voyennaya nauka* [Soviet military science]. Moscow: Znaniya.

————. 1988. "Great October and Defense of the Motherland." *Oktyabr* [October] 2 (February).

Glagolev, V. 1988. "Christianity Today and the Struggle Against the War Danger." *International Affairs* 2.

Glebov, Ivan. 1988. "USSR and India: Cooperation in the Interests of Progress & Peace." *International Affairs* 2 (February).

Gorbachev, M. S. 1985. *A Time for Peace.* New York: Richardson & Steirman.

————. 1986a. *Political Report of the Central Committee to the 27th Congress of the CPSU.* Novosti Press Agency, February 25.

————. 1986b. *Speeches and Writings.* Oxford: Pergamon Press.

————. 1986c. *The Coming Century of Peace.* New York: Richardson & Steirman.

————. 1986d. "Vladivostok Speech," 28 July 1986. BBC Monitoring Service.

————. 1986e. "Vremia trebuyet novogo politecheskogo myshlenia" [The age demands new political thinking]. *Kommunist* 16 (November).

————. 1987a. *Perestroika: New Thinking for Our Country and the World.* New York: Harper & Row.

————. 1987b. "Realnost i garantii bezopasnogo mira." *Pravda,* 17 September; reprinted: "Reality and Guarantees for a Secure World," *International Affairs* 11.

————. 1987c. *Izbrannye rechi i stati* [Selected speeches and articles]. Moscow: Izd. politicheskoi literatury.

————. 1987d. *Toward a Better World.* New York: Richardson & Steirman.

————. 1987e. "For a Nuclear-Free World, for Humanism in International Relations." Address to the International Forum for a Nuclear-Free World. *Pravda*, February 17; reprinted in CDSP 39, 7.

————. 1987f. Address at the 70th Anniversary of the Great October Revolution. *Pravda*, November 3; reprinted in CDSP 39, 44 (2 December).

————. 1987g. "USSR-CSSR: Bonds of Fraternal Friendship." *Pravda*, 10 April; reprinted in CDSP 39, 15.

————. 1988a. "Revolutionary Perestroika and the Ideology of Renewal." Speech at the Plenary Meeting of the CPSU Central Committee, February 18; reprinted in *Moscow News*, Supplement, No. 9.

————. 1988b. Address to the Foundation for the Survival and Development of Humanity. *Pravda*, 15 January; reprinted in *Moscow News* 5.

————. 1988c. Report on progress in implementation of the resolutions of the 27th CPSU Congress to the 19th All-Union CPSU Conference. *Pravda*, 28 June; reprinted in *Moscow News* 27.

————. 1988d. "Moschnyi factor mirovoi politiki" [A mighty factor of world politics]. *Pravda*, 4 July.

————. 1988e. "Time for Action, Time for Practical Work" [the Krasnoyarsk speech]. *Pravda*, 18 September; reprinted in FBIS-SOV-88-182.

————. 1988f. Address to the 43rd Session of the UNO. *Pravda*, 7 December.

————. 1988g. Answers questions from *The Washington Post* and *Newsweek. Moscow News*; reprinted from *Pravda*, 23 May 1988.

————. 1989. Speech at a meeting with working people in the city of Kiev [the Kiev speech]. *Krasnaya zvezda*, 23 February; reprinted in FBIS-SOV-89-036, 24 February.

Grachev, N. 1988. "Nuclear War and Its Consequences." *International Affairs* 3 (March).

Gromyko, A. A. 1988. "Security for All in the Nuclear Age." In Gromyko and Hellman, eds.

Gromyko, A., and Hellman, M., eds. 1988. *Breakthrough/Proryv: Emerging New Thinking: Soviet and Western Scholars Issue Challenge to Build a World Beyond War.* New York: Walker.

Gromyko, A., and Lomeiko, V. 1984. *Novoe myshlenie v yadernyi vek* [New thinking in the nuclear age]. Moscow: Mezhdunarodnye otnoshenia.

Gvishiani, D. 1979. "Globalnye problemy i globalnoe modelirovanie" [Global problems and global modeling]. *MEMO* 3.

Ivanov, I. 1987a. "The Conception of Interconnection between Disarmament and Development." *MEMO* 8.

————. 1987b. "Demilitarizaciia mirovoy ekonomiki—nasushchaia neob-khodimost" [The demilitarization of the world economy—the real necessity]. *MEMO* 8.

Ivanov, L. 1988. "Nuclear Weapons and West European 'Defense'—New Thinking versus Old Concepts." *Pravda*, 29 November; reprinted in FBIS-SOV-88-230, 30 November.

Ivanov, Vilen. 1987. "A Nuclear-Free World and Social Consciousness." *Kommunist* 5; reprinted in *Soviet Law and Government* 31, 3 (Winter 1987–88).

Izyumov, A. 1988. "The Other Side of Disarmament." *International Affairs* 3.

Izyumov, A., and Kortunov, A. 1988. "The Soviet Union in the Changing World." *International Affairs* 8 (August).

Kanevsky, Boris, and Shabardin, Pyotr. 1988. "The Correlation of Politics, War and Nuclear Catastrophe." *International Affairs* 2.

Kapchenko, N. 1984. "The Marxist-Leninist Methodology of Analyzing International Relations and Foreign Policy." *International Affairs* 7 (July).

————. 1987a. "Sovetskaia koncepciia mira v svete istoricheskogo opyta Oktiabria" [The Soviet conception of the world in the light of the historical experience of October]. *MEMO* 10.

————. 1987b. "The Political Philosophy of Peace in the Nuclear-Missile Age." *International Affairs* 3 (March).

Karaganov, S. E. 1988. "The Military Aspect of the 'Common European Home.'" *Mezhdunarodnaya zhizn* 7; reprinted in JPRS-UMA-88-023, 29 September.

Karasev, N. 1988. "SOI i novoe myshlenie: logika razviazok." *Pravda*, 20 April.

Karlov, Yuri. 1988. "The Moral Factor in World Politics." *International Affairs* 3.

Khachaturov, Karen. 1988. "A Rebellious Church." *International Affairs* 4 (April).

Kim, M. 1988. "Leninizm i istoricheskie sudby socializma: Voprosy teorii" [Leninism and the historical destiny of socialism: questions of theory]. *Pravda*, 5 February.

Kirshin, Y. Y. 1987. "The Philosophy of Forming the Secure World." *Voprosy filosofii* 4.

Kokoshin, A. 1988. "From the Standpoint of the New Thinking: Three Major Elements of Stability." *Krasnaya zvezda* 16 (September); reprinted in FBIS-SOV-88-183, 21 September.

"Kommunike zasedania Komiteta ministrov inostrannykh del gosudarstv—uchastnikov Varshavskogo Dogovora" [The communique of the meeting of foreign ministers of the members of the Warsaw Treaty]. 1988. *Pravda*, 31 March.

Kondrashov, S. 1988. "Ends and Means, or a Digression into History Prompted by Current Events." *Izvestiya*, 15 December; reprinted in FBIS-SOV-88-243, 19 December.

Konobeyev, V. 1988. "The Benefits of Converting Arms Production." *International Affairs* 2 (February).

Konstantinov, Yuri. 1988. "Can the Ruble Become a Convertible Currency?" *International Affairs* 3 (March).

Kortunov, V. 1986. "Novoe politicheskoe myshlenie—imperativ sovremennosti" [New political thinking—the imperative of our time]. *MEMO* 10.

————. 1987. "A Revolutionary Change in the Thinking of Millions." *International Affairs* 11 (November).

————. 1988. "Realism and Morality in Politics." In Gromyko and Hellman, eds.

Kozyrev, A. V. 1988. "Doverie i balans interesov" [Trust and the balance of interests]. *Mezhdunarodnaya zhizn* 10; reprinted in *New York Times*, 7 January 1989.

Krasin, I. 1986. "Strategiia mira—imperativ epokhi" [Peace strategy—the imperative of the epoch]. *MEMO* 1.

————. 1988a. "A esli bez militarizma? Mozhet li kapitalizm prisposobitsu k beziadernomu miru?" [And without the militarism? Can capitalism adjust to the nuclear-free world?]. *Pravda*, January 28.

————. 1988b. "Rabochee dvizhenie v poiskakh demokraticheskoi alternativy" [The working class movement in search of a democratic alternative]. *Kommunist* 14 (September).

————. 1988c. "Novoe myshlenie vo vzaimootnosheniiakh kommunistov i social-demokratov" [New thinking in the mutual relations of communists and social democrats]. *MEMO* 4.

Krychkov, V. 1988. "Viewing the World Objectively." *International Affairs* 11 (November).

Kuzmin, V. P. 1986. "The Rise of the Communist Social Formation." *Voprosy filosofii* 6.

Kuznetsov, V. 1988. "A European Home: What Will It Be Like?" *Pravda*, 15 October; reprinted in FBIS-SOV-88-203, 20 October.

Lebedev, Y., and Podberezkin, A. 1988. "Voennye doktriny i mezhdunarodnaia bezopasnost" [Military doctrines and international security]. *Kommunist* 13 (September).

Ligachev, Y. 1986. "Kursom oktiabria v dukhe revolucionnogo tvorchestva" [On the October path in the spirit of revolutionary achievement]. *Pravda*, 7 November.

————. 1987. "The Revolutionary Essence of Perestroika." *World Marxist Review* 30, 7 (July).

Lizichev, A. D. 1987. "Oktiabr i leninskoe uchenie o zashchite revolutsii" [The October and Leninist teaching on the defense of the revolution]. *Kommunist* 3.

Lomeiko, V. 1988. "Krushenie mifov" [The dismantling of myths]. *Pravda*, 15 March.

Lyutov, Ivan. 1988. "Lenin's Ideas on Defending Socialism and Evolution of the Military Doctrine." *International Affairs* 3 (March).

Maklyarsky, B. M., ed. 1987. *Sovremennyi mir glazami "zelenykh"* [The contemporary world through the eyes of the Greenies]. Moscow: Mezhdunavodnye Otnoshenia.

Markov, M. A. 1977. "Nauchilis li my myslit po novomu?" [Have we learned to think new?]. *Voprosy filosofii* 8.

Marushkin, B. 1988. "Novoe myshlenie i sovremennyi mir: preodolet 'obraz vraga'" [New thinking in the contemporary world: to overcome the "image of an enemy"]. *Pravda*, 6 January.

"Marxist-Leninist Studies Called Upon to Educate Active Fighters for Restructuring." 1988. *Pravda*, 5 October; reprinted in FBIS-SOV-88-194, 6 October.

Medvedev, V. 1988a. "Velikij Oktiabr i sovremennyi mir" [The great October revolution and the contemporary world]. *Kommunist* 2.

————. 1988b. "The Contemporary Concept of Socialism." *Pravda*, 5 October; reprinted in FBIS-SOV-88-194, 6 October.

Melville, A. Y. 1988. "Nuclear Revolution and the New Way of Thinking." In Gromyko and Hellman, eds.

Mikhailov, N. 1988. "Poasnyi arkhaizm: 'Germanskii vopros' i novoe myshlenie" [A dangerous anachronism: 'the German question' and new thinking]. *Pravda*, 24 April.

Molov, O. 1989. "From the Position of the New Thinking" 'Chemical Zero': Who Is Against?" *Krasnaya zvezda* 5 (January); reprinted in FBIS-SOV-89-004, 6 January.

Morozov, G. 1986. "Mirovoe soobshchestvo i sud'by mira" [Peaceful coexistence and the destiny of the world]. *MEMO* 10.

Mostovets, A. 1988. "To Cut Off the Military Branch." *International Affairs* 4 (April).

Mshvenieradze, V. 1986. "New Political Thinking." *Sotsiologicheskie issledovaniia* 3; reprinted in *Soviet Law and Government* 26, 2 (Fall 1987).

"Neotlozhnaia problema sovremennosti" [A present age question that cannot be postponed]. 1987. *MEMO* 8.

"Novoe politicheskoe myshlenie v deistvii" [New political thinking in action]. 1986. *Kommunist* 13.

Nikitin, A. I. 1988. "The Concept of Universal Security: A Revolution of Thinking and Policy in the Nuclear Age." In Gromyko and Hellman, eds.

"October Revolution, Peace, Peaceful Coexistence" [round table]. 1987. *New Times*, 9 November.

Ovchinnikov, V. 1989. "Interdependence and Security: The Speech at the United Nations, Impetus for Search and Action." *Pravda*, 5 January; reprinted in FBIS-SOV-89-007, 11 January.

Pankin, A. 1988. "We Cannot Do without Self-criticism and Self-analysis" (A reply to Antonovich). *International Affairs* 6 (June).

Pantin, I. 1987. "October and the Development of Mankind." *Pravda*, 23 October; reprinted in CDSP 39, 43.

"Perestroika, the 19th Party Conference and Foreign Policy." 1988. *International Affairs* 7 (July).

Petrovsky, V. 1985. "The UN: An Instrument of Joint Action in the Interest of Peace." *International Affairs*, October.

—————. 1986. "Sovetskaia koncepciia vseobshchei bezopasnosti" [The Soviet conception of global security]. *MEMO* 10.

—————. 1988. "OON i obnovlenie mira" [The UN and the renewal of the world]. *MEMO* 4.

Plimak, E. G. 1986. "Marksizm-Leninizm i revolucionnost konca XX veka" [Marxism-Leninism and revolutionism at the end of the 20th century]. *Pravda* 14 November.

—————. 1987. "Novoe myshlenie: perspektivy socialnogo obnovlenia mira" [New thinking—perspectives on the social renewal of the world]. *Voprosy filosofii* 6.

Pokrokovsky, A. 1988. "Stock Markets in Turmoil." *International Affairs* 2 (February).

Pozdniakov, E. 1988. "Nacionalnye, gosudarstvennye i klasovye interesy v mezhdunarodnykh otnosheniakh" [National, state and class interests in international relations]. *MEMO* 5.

Primakov, E. 1986a. "XXVII s'ezd KPSS i islledovanie problem mirovoi ekonomiki i mezhdunarodnykh otnoshenii" [The 27th CPSU Congress and the study of problems of world economy and international relations]. *MEMO* 5.

—————. 1986b. "Put' v budushchee" [The road to the future]. *Pravda*, 22 January.

—————. 1987a. "Novaia filosofiia vneshnei politiki." *Pravda*, 10 July; English translation as "New 'Flexibility' in Soviet Foreign Policy," *Current Digest of the Soviet Press* 39, 28 (12 August 1987).

—————. 1987b. "In the same boat." *New Times*, 26 October.

—————. 1987c. "Kapitalizm vo vzaimosviazannov mire" [Capitalism in the interdependent world]. *Kommunist* 13.

—————. 1988a. "USSR Policy on Regional Conflicts." *International Affairs* 6 (June).

—————. 1988b. "A Look into the Past and the Future." CDSP 40, 1.

Proektor, D. 1988a. "Politics, Clausewitz and Victory in a Nuclear War." *International Affairs* 3 (March).

—————. 1988b. "Balance of Power; Authority or Loss of Authority?" *Literaturnaia gazeta*, 9 November; reprinted in FBIS-SOV-88-218, 10 November.

Pryakhin, V. 1988. "New Means in the Practice of Diplomatic Negotiations." *International Affairs* 1.

Rakhmaninov, Yuri. 1988. "Europe: Approaching the Third Millennium." *International Affairs* 4 (April).

Razoruzhenie i bezopasnost—1986, Ezhegodnik [Disarmament and security—1986, yearbook]. 1987. 2 volumes. Moscow: Novosti.

"Reason Demands New Political Thinking." 1987. *Voprosy istorii,* 10; reprinted in *Soviet Law and Government* 31, 1 (Summer).

"Resolutions Adopted by the 42nd Session of the UN General Assembly: A Comprehensive System of International Peace and Security." 1988. *International Affairs* 4 (April).

"Rezolucii 19th vsesojuznoi konferencii" [Resolutions of the 19th all-union conference]. 1988. *Pravda,* 5 July.

Rodachin, V. 1989. "Why the Orwellian Language Here?" *Krasnaya zvezda,* 7 February; reprinted in FBIS-SOV-89-030.

Rogov, S. 1988. "SSSR-SShA: balans sil ili balans interesov?" [The USSR-USA: the balance of power or balance of interests?]. *Pravda,* 14 June.

Rubinsky, Yuri. 1988. "European Community: Political Dimensions." *International Affairs* 2 (February).

Rzheshevstkiy, O. A., and Gaddis, J. L. 1988. "Two Views of a Single Problem." *Pravda,* 31 October; reprinted in FBIS-SOV-88-213, 3 November.

Sanakoev, Sh. 1987. "A Comprehensive International Security System and the Realities of the Nuclear and Space Era." *International Affairs* 1 (January).

———. 1988. "Peaceful Coexistence in the Context of Military-Strategic Parity." *International Affairs* 2 (February).

Selyaninov, O. 1987. "Lenin on the Connection between Domestic and Foreign Policy." *International Affairs* 10 (October).

Semeyko, L. 1989. "Toward Strategic Stability." *Krasnaya zvezda,* 21 February; reprinted in FBIS-SOV-89-034, 22 February.

Semyonov, Vsevolod. 1988. "A New Situation in Afghanistan." *International Affairs* 4 (April).

Serebryannikov, V. 1988. "National Security in the Nuclear Age." *Kommunist vooruzhennykh sil* 9 (May); reprinted in JPRS-UMA-88-023, 29 September.

"Seven Decades—the Judgment of History." 1988. *International Affairs* 1 (January).

Shakhnazarov, G. K. 1981. *Gradushchij miroporiadok* [The coming world order]. Moscow.

———. 1983. *Sotsializm i budushchee* [Socialism and the future]. Moscow.

———. 1984. "Logika Politicheskogo myshlenia v yadernuyu eru" [The logic of political thinking in the nuclear age]. *Voprosy filosofii* 5.

———. 1986. "Internacionalizacia—istoki, soderzhanie, stupeni razvitia" [Globalization—sources, meaning, stage of development]. *MEMO* 5.

————. 1988a. "Mirovoe soobschchestvo upravliaemo" [Governability of the world society]. *Pravda*, 15 January.

————. 1988b. "Governability of the World." *International Affairs* 3 (March).

————. 1988c. "Science on Politics. Notes From the 14th World Congress in Washington." *Pravda*, 26 September; reprinted in FBIS-SOV-88-189, 29 September.

Shashkov, Yevgeni. 1988. "The Strategy of Acceleration and the Historical Destiny of Socialism." *International Affairs* 1 (January).

Shevardnadze, E. 1988a. "Pismo ministra inostrannykh del SSSR generalnomu sekretariu OON po voprosu obespecheniia doveriia, rasshirenia otkrytosti i glasnosti v vojennoj oblasti" [A letter of the Foreign Minister to the UN General Secretary on the question of ensuring trust, broadening openness and glasnost in the military area]. *Pravda*, 11 June.

————. 1988b. "Vystuplenie, Tretia specialnaia sessia Generalnoi Assamblei OON po razoruzheniu" [Address to the Third Special Session of the General Assembly of the UN]. *Pravda*, 9 June.

————. 1988c. "Striving for Comprehensive Security. Speech at the 43rd UN General Assembly Session." *Pravda*, 28 September; reprinted in FBIS-SOV-99-188, 28 September.

————. 1989. "Address to the final follow-up meeting of the Conference on Security and Cooperation in Europe." TASS, 19 January; reprinted in FBIS-SOV-89-012, 19 January.

Shiryaev, Yuri. 1988. "CMEA; Restructuring the Multilateral Cooperation Mechanism." *International Affairs* 1 (January).

Simoniya, N. 1989. "UN Speech: Boost for Quest and Action. Principle of Freedom of Choice." *Pravda*, 18 January; reprinted in FBIS-SOV-89-017.

Smirnov, G. 1987. "The Revolutionary Essence of Renewal." *Pravda*, March 13; reprinted in CDSP 39, 11.

"Soveshchanie vneshnepoliticheskikh rabotnikov" [The meeting of the workers in the field of foreign affairs]. 1986. *Pravda*, May 24.

"Soviet-Yugoslav Declaration." 1988. *Pravda*, 19 March; reprinted in FBIS-SOV-88-054, 21 March.

Stanislavlev, Andrei, and Tuzmukhamedov, Bakhtiyar. 1988. "This Seemed Unattainable." *International Affairs* 3 (March).

"Statement of the Warsaw Pact Defence Ministers Committee: On the Correlation of Warsaw Pact and North Atlantic Treaty Alliance Force Strengths and Armament in Europe and Adjoining Waters." 1989. *Pravda*, 30 January; reprinted in FBIS-SOV-89-018, 30 January.

"The Soviet Union in an Interdependent World." 1988. *International Affairs* 3 (March).

"The Washington Prologue." 1988. *International Affairs* 4 (April).

"Theses of the CPSU for the 19th All-Union Conference of the CPSU." 1988. *Pravda*, 27 May; reprinted in *Moscow News* 23.

Tkachuk, Boris, and Tumalaryav, Vladimir. 1988. "A Cause for Reflection." *International Affairs* 3 (March).

Tomashevsky, D., and Lukov, V. 1985. "Interesy chelovechestva i mirovaya politika" [The interests of humanity and world politics]. *MEMO* 4.

Trofimenko, G. A. 1987. "Novye real'nosti i novoe myshlenie" [New realities and new thinking]. *SShA* 2.

Usachev, I. G. 1988. "Universal and Class Foundations in World Politics." *Kommunist* 11 (July); reprinted in JPRS-UKO-88-017, 27 October.

"V XXI vek—bez iadernogo oruzhia: centralnoe napravlenie nashei vneshnei politiki" [Into the 21st century—without nuclear weapons: the main direction of our foreign policy]. 1988. *Pravda*, 15 January.

Vakhrameyev, A. 1988. "Perestroika is still in its early stage." *International Affairs* 3 (March).

Vasilev, G. 1988. "Snova stereotipy 'kholodnoi voiny'" [Once again the stereotypes of the "cold war"]. *Pravda*, 15 January.

Venyaminova, M. 1988. "USSR and UNESCO: Prospects for Cooperation." *International Affairs* 2 (February).

Vereshchetin, V. S., and Miullerson, R. A. 1988. "Pravo, a ne sila" [Law not force]. *Pravda*, 2 April.

Vladimirov, O. 1985. "The Main Element in the International Revolutionary Process." *Pravda*, 21 June.

Vladmirsky, P. 1987. "Comprehensive Security Equal for All." *International Affairs* 10 (October).

Volskiy, D. 1988. "We and the 'Third World' through the Prism of Modern Thinking." *Izvestiya*, 22 December; reprinted in FBIS-SOV-88-247, 23 December.

Voronin, Aleksei. 1988. "Perfecting Diplomatic Practice." *International Affairs* 1 (January).

"Vremia trebuet novogo myshlenia" [The time demands new thinking]. 1986. *Kommunist* 16 (November); reprinted in CDSP 39, 28 (12 August 1987).

Yakovlev, A. 1986. "Mezhduimperialisticheskie protivorechia—sovremennyi kontekst" [Interimperialist contradictions—the contemporary context]. *Kommunist* 17 (November).

———. 1987. "Dostizhenie kachestvenno novogo sostoiania sovetskogo obshchestva i obshchestvennye nauki" [The achievement of a qualitatively new stage of Soviet society and the social sciences]. *Kommunist* 8 (May).

———. 1989. "Yakovlev Interview on Restructuring, Disarmament." *Der Spiegel*, 16 January; reprinted in FBIS-SOV-89-010, 17 January.

Yazov, D. T. 1988a. "The Military Balance of Strength and Nuclear Missile Parity." *International Affairs* 4 (April).

————. 1988b. "O voennom balanse sil i raketnoiadernom paritete" [On the military balance of forces and missile parity]. *Pravda*, 8 March; reprinted in *Moscow News* Supplement, 1988/8.

————. 1988c. "Vo imia mira i bezopasnosti" [In the name of peace and security]. *Pravda*, 30 April.

Zagladin, V. 1985. "World Balance of Forces and the Development of International Relations (Aspects of Theory and Methodology)." *International Affairs* 3 (March).

————. 1986a. "Programnye tseli KPSS i globalnye problemy" [Programmatic goals of the CPSU and global problems]. *Voprosy filosofii* 2; reprinted in *Soviet Law and Government* 25, 2 (Fall 1986).

————. 1986b. "Velichie revolucionnoy teorii" [The greatness of revolutionary theory]. *MEMO* 3.

————. 1988a. "Kurzom razuma i gumanizma" [Following reason and humanism]. *Pravda*, 13 June.

————. 1988b. "No Need to Fear Similarity: Reflections on the Interdependence of the World." *Moscow News* 22.

Zagladin, V. V., and Frolov, I. T. 1981. *Globalnye problemy sovremennosti: nauchnyi i socialnyi aspekty* [Contemporary global problems: scientific and social aspects]. Moscow.

Zagorsky, A. 1987. "The Hard Road to New Thinking." *International Affairs* 8 (August).

————. 1988. "The Way to Security: Polish Initiative." *International Affairs* 1 (January).

"Zapad takzhe dolzhen myslit po-novomu" [The West also needs to think new]. 1988. *Kommunist* 12 (August).

Zhdanov, Yu. 1987. "Klassovoe i obshchechelovecheskoe v yadernyi vek [Class and all-human in the nuclear age]. *Pravda* 6 (March).

Zhukov, Y., and Melnikov, I. 1984. "An Imperative: Actions Capable of Making a Durable Peace a Reality." *International Affairs* 7 (July).

Zhurkin, V.; Karaganov, S.; and Kortunov, A. 1987. "Reasonable Sufficiency—or How to Break the Vicious Circle." *New Times* 40.

————, ————, and ————. 1988. "Vyzovy bezopasnosti-starye i novye" [Challenges to security: old and new]. *Kommunist* 1.

Appendix 2

SELECTED BIBLIOGRAPHY OF
WESTERN ANALYSES OF "NEW THINKING"

Adornato, F. 1989. "An Interview with PCI Secretary General Achille Occhetto." *L'Espresso*, 29 January; reprinted in FBIS-WEU-89-033.

Arnold, Anthony. 1987. "Perspectives on Afghanistan." *Problems of Communism* 36, 5 (September–October).

Aslund, Anders. 1988. "The New Soviet Policy towards International Economic Organizations." *The World Today* 44, 2 (February).

Balzer, H. D. 1985. "Is Less More? Soviet Science in the Gorbachev Era." *Issues in Science and Technology* 1, 4.

Battle, J. M. 1988. "Uskorenie, Glasnost, and Perestroika: The Pattern of Reform under Gorbachev." *Soviet Studies* 50, 3 (July).

Bechtoldt, Heinrich. 1987. "Gorbachev: Initiatives or Reactions?" *Aussenpolitik* 38, 4.

Berner, Wolfgang, and Dahm, Helmut. 1987. *"Neues Denken" in der Aussenpolitik der UDSSR. Mit Dokumentation*. Berichte des Bundesinstituts für ostwissenschaftliche und internationale Studien, 46.

Besancon, A. 1989. "Should We Help Gorbachev?" *Le Figaro*, 11 January; reprinted in FBIS-WEU-89-034, 22 February.

Bialer, Seweryn. 1986. *The Soviet Paradox: External Expansion, Internal Decline*. London: Tauris & Co.

————. 1987. "Gorbachev's Move." *Foreign Policy* 68 (Fall).

————. 1988. "Gorbachev's Program of Change: Sources, Significance, Prospects." *Political Science Quarterly* 103, 3.

Bialer, S., and Afferica, J. 1986. "The Genesis of Gorbachev's World." *Foreign Affairs* 64, 3.

Blackwell, Robert D. 1988. "Conceptual Problems of Conventional Arms Control." *International Security* 12, 4 (Spring).

Bowie, R. R. 1987. "Gorbachev's International Agenda." *Christian Science Monitor*, 27 November.

Brown, Archie. 1985. "Gorbachev's Policy Innovations." *Bulletin of Atomic Scientists* 41, 10 (November).

————. 1986a. "The Future in His Hands." *Times Literary Supplement*, 18 July.

————. 1986b. "Change in the Soviet Union." *Foreign Affairs* 64, 5 (Summer).

————. 1986c. "Political Science in the USSR." *International Political Science Review* 7, 4 (October).

————. 1987a. "Gorbachev and Reform of the Soviet System." *Political Quarterly* 58, 2 (April–June).

————. 1987b. "Soviet Political Developments and Prospects." *World Policy Journal*, Winter.

————. 1987c. "A Performer in the Kremlin." *The Nation*, 13 June.

Brzezinski, Z. 1984. "The Soviet Union: World Power of a New Type." *The Soviet Union in the 1980's: Proceedings of the Academy of Political Science.*

————. 1988a. "US Foreign Policy in the Post-Reagan Era." *IPA Review* 42, 1 (May–July).

————. 1988b. "America's New Geostrategy." *Foreign Affairs* 66, 4 (Spring).

————. 1988c. "Still no trust, but . . ." *Moscow News*, May 8.

————. 1989. *The Grand Failure: The Birth and Death of Communism in the Twentieth Century.* New York: Scribners.

Bukovsky, V. 1989. "Who Resists Gorbachev?" *Washington Quarterly*, Winter.

Bunce, V. 1986. "The Effects of Leadership Succession in the Soviet Union." *American Political Science Review* 80, 1 (March).

Caldwell, Lawrence T. 1987. "United States–Soviet Relations and Arms Control." *Current History* 86, 522 (October).

Casey, William J. 1987. "Focus on the Third World: Challenges and Opportunities." *Presidential Studies Quarterly* 17, 1 (Winter).

Challenges of Our Time: Disarmament and Social Progress. 1986. New York: International Publishers.

Chase, James. 1988. "A New Grand Strategy." *Foreign Policy* 70 (Spring).

Checinski, M. 1987. "Warsaw Pact/CEMA Military-Economic Trends." *Problems of Communism*, March–April.

Cockburn, P. 1988/89. "Gorbachev and Soviet Conservatism." *World Policy Journal*, Winter.

Cohen, S. F. 1987. "Sovieticus." *The Nation*, 13 June.

Colton, T. J. 1985. "The Soviet Union under Gorbachev." *Current History* 84, 504.

————. 1986. *Dilemma of Reform in the Soviet Union.* New York: Council on Foreign Relations.

Conquest, R. 1986. "Dissent in the Soviet Union." In Dallin and Rice, eds.

Croan, Melvin. 1986. "Last Stages of Leninism." *Problems of Communism* 35, 1 (January–February).

Curtis, C., ed. 1983. *The Challenge of Soviet Shipping.* London: Aims of Industry.

Daggett, Stephen, and English, Robert D. 1988. "Assessing Soviet Strategic Defense." *Foreign Policy* 70 (Spring).

Dallin, Alexander. 1986. "A Soviet Master Plan." In Dallin and Rice, eds.

Dallin, A., and Rice, Condolezza, eds. 1986. *The Gorbachev Era*. Stanford: Stanford Alumni Association.

Dawisha, K. 1986. "Gorbachev and Eastern Europe: A New Challenge for the West?" *World Policy Journal* 3, 2.

Dawisha, K., and Valdez, J. 1987. "Socialist Internationalism in Eastern Europe." *Problems of Communism*, March–April.

Douglass, J. D. 1988. *Why the Soviets Violate Arms Control Treaties*. Washington: Pergamon Brassey's.

Duffy, Gloria, and Lee, Jennifer. 1988. "The Soviet Debate on 'Reasonable Sufficiency.'" *Arms Control Today*, October.

Eberstadt, N. 1987. "The Latest Myths about the Soviet Union." *Commentary*, May.

Evangelista, Matthew. 1987. "'New Thinking' in Foreign Policy." *The Nation*, 13 June.

Evans, Alfred Jr. 1986. "The Decline of Developed Socialism? Some Trends in Recent Soviet Ideology." *Soviet Studies* 38, 1 (January).

Frank, Peter. 1987. "Gorbachev and the 'Psychological Restructuring' of Soviet Society." *The World Today*, May.

Fukuyama, Francis. 1986. "Gorbachev and the Third World." *Foreign Affairs*, Spring.

————. 1987. "Patterns of Soviet Third World Policy." *Problems of Communism* 36, 5 (September–October).

Gati, C. 1988/89. "Eastern Europe on Its Own." *Foreign Affairs* 68, 1.

Gelman, H. 1986. "Gorbachev's Dilemmas and His Conflicting Foreign-Policy Goals." *Orbis* 30/2 (Summer).

Gill, G. 1987. "A Gorbachev Revolution?: Soviet 'Openness' in Action." *Current Affairs Bulletin*, June.

Glickham, C. 1986. "New Directions in Soviet Foreign Policy." *Radio Liberty Research Bulletin*, Supplement 2/86, 6 September.

Glynn, Patrick. 1988. "Reagan's Rush to Disarm." *Commentary*, March.

Golan, Galia. 1987. "Moscow and Third World National Liberation Movements: The Soviet Role." *Journal of International Affairs* 40, 2 (Winter/Spring).

Goldberg, A. C. 1988. "Moscow's New Military Doctrine: A Tamer Bear?" *Washington Times*, October.

Goldman, M. I., and Goldman, M. 1987/88. "Soviet and Chinese Economic Reform." *Foreign Affairs* 66, 3.

Goure, L. 1988. "A 'New' Soviet Military Doctrine: Reality or Mirage?" *Strategic Review*, Summer.

Griffith, Franklyn. 1986. "Current Soviet Military Doctrine." *National Security Issues of the USSR*, North Atlantic Treaty Organization workshop, 6–7 November. Martinus Nijhoff.

Gross, Natalie. 1987. "Glasnost: Roots and Practice." *Problems of Communism* 36 (November–December).

Gustafson, Thane, and Mann, Dawn. 1986. "Gorbachev's First Year: Building Power and Authority." *Problems of Communism* 35 (May–June).

————, and ————. 1987. "Gorbachev's Next Gamble." *Problems of Communism* 36, 4 (July–August).

Halliday, F. 1987. "Gorbachev and the 'Arab Syndrome': Soviet Policy in the Middle East." *World Policy Journal* 4, 3 (Summer).

Hanson, Philip. 1987. "Reforming the Foreign-Trade System." *Radio Liberty Research Bulletin*, RL 104/87, 19 March.

Harasymiw, B. 1988. "The CPSU in Transition from Brezhnev to Gorbachev." *Canadian Journal of Political Science/Revue canadienne de science politique* 21, 2 (June/juin).

Hasegawa, Tsuyoshi. 1986. "Soviets on Nuclear War-Fighting." *Problems of Communism* 35 (July–August).

————. 1987. "The New Thinking and Gorbachev's Foreign Military Policy." Tokyo. May.

Healey, D. 1987. "A Labour Britain, NATO and the Bomb." *Foreign Affairs* 65, 4 (Spring).

Herspring, Dale R. 1987. "Gorbachev, Yazov, and the Military." *Problems of Communism*, 36, 4 (July–August).

Hofheinz, P. 1987. "Gorbachev's Double Burden: Economic Reform and Growth Acceleration." *Millennium* 16, 1.

Holloway, D. 1988/89. "Gorbachev's New Thinking." *Foreign Affairs* 68, 1.

Horn, R. C. 1987. "Soviet Leadership Changes and Sino-Soviet Relations." *Orbis* 30, 4 (Winter).

Hough, Jerry F. 1985. "Gorbachev's Strategy." *Foreign Affairs* 64, 1.

————. 1986. *The Struggle for the Third World: Soviet Debates and American Options*. Washington, D.C.: Brookings Institution.

————. 1987. "Gorbachev Consolidating Power." *Problems of Communism* 36, 4 (July–August).

Howard, Michael. 1987/88. "Russia Rethinks the Revolution." *The World Today*, November.

————. 1988. "A European Perspective on the Reagan Years." *Foreign Affairs* 66, 3.

Huntington, Samuel P. 1987/88. "Coping with the Lippmann Gap." *Foreign Affairs* 66, 3.

Hyland, W. G. 1985. "The Gorbachev Succession." *Foreign Affairs* 63 (September).

————. 1987. "Reagan-Gorbachev III." *Foreign Affairs* 66, 1 (Fall).

Jancar, Barbara. 1987. *Environmental Management in the Soviet Union and Yugoslavia*. Durham, N.C.: Duke University Press.

Janson, Charles. 1986. "The Power of Unbelief." *Soviet Analyst* 15, 25 (17 December).

————. 1987. "Marxism/Leninism and After." *Soviet Analyst* 16, 16 (August).

Jenisch, Uwe. 1988. "The Future of the UN Law of the Sea Convention." *Aussenpolitik* 39, 1.

Kaiser, Karl. 1988. "Conventional Arms Control: The Future Agenda." *The World Today*, 44, 2 (February).

Kaiser, R. G. 1988/89. "The U.S.S.R. in Decline." *Foreign Affairs* 67, 2.

Kaminski, B., and Janes, R. W. 1988. "Eastern Europe and the Third World." *Problems of Communism*, March–April.

Katseneliboigen, A. 1988. "Will Glasnost Bring the Reactionaries to Power?" *Orbis* 32, 2 (Spring).

Kennedy, P. 1987. "What Gorbachev Is Up Against." *Atlantic Monthly* 259, 6 (June).

Kintner, W. R. 1987. *Soviet Global Strategy*. Fairfax, Va.: Hero Books.

Kissinger, H. A. 1988. "Observations on U.S.-Soviet Relations." *Heritage Lectures*, 14 January.

Korbonski, A., and Fukuyama F., eds. 1987. *The Soviet Union and the Third World: The Last Three Decades*. London: Cornell University Press.

Kubálková, V. 1988. "Soviet 'New Thinking' on International Relations." Lecture series, Stanford University, January 25, 26, 28.

Kubálková, V., and Cruickshank, A. A. 1989. *Marxism and International Relations*. Oxford: Oxford Paperback.

Kusin, V. V. 1986. "Gorbachev and Eastern Europe." *Problems of Communism* 35, 1 (January–February).

Laird, Roy D. 1987. "Perestroika and Soviet Agriculture." *Problems of Communism* 36, 6 (November–December).

Lambeth, B., and Lewis, K. 1988. "The Kremlin and SDI." *Foreign Affairs* 66, 4 (Spring).

Lapidus, Gail W. 1987. "Gorbachev and the Reform of the Soviet System." *Daedalus*, Spring.

Larrabee, F. Stephen. 1988a. "Eastern Europe: A Generational Change." *Foreign Policy* 70 (Spring).

————. 1988b. "Gorbachev and the Soviet Military." *Foreign Affairs* 66, 5 (Summer).

Larrabee, F. S., and Lynch, A. 1986–87. "Gorbachev: The Road to Reykjavik." *Foreign Affairs* 65 (Winter).

Lavigne, Marie. 1986. "Problems Facing the Soviet Economy." In Dallin and Rice, eds.

Laqueur, W. 1983. "What We Know About the Soviet Union." *Commentary* 75, 2 (February).

Legvold, Robert. 1988. "The Emerging Revolution in Soviet Policy." Colin Miller Lecture, Berkeley, 25 February.

————. 1988/89. "The Revolution in Soviet Foreign Policy." *Foreign Affairs* 68, 1.

Legvold, Robert, and the Task Force on Soviet New Thinking. 1988. *Gorbachev's Foreign Policy: How Should the United States Respond?* Headline Series No. 284, Foreign Policy Association, April.

Leonhard, Wolfgang. 1987–88. "The Bolshevik Revolution Turns 70." *Foreign Affairs*, Winter.

Lewin, M. 1988. *The Gorbachev Phenomenon: A Historical Interpretation.* Berkeley: University of California Press.

Light, M. 1987a. "'New Thinking' in Soviet Foreign Policy." *Coexistence* 24, 3.

————. 1987b. "The Study of International Relations in the Soviet Union." *Millennium* 16, 2.

————. 1988. *The Soviet Theory of International Relations.* London: Wheatsheaf Books.

Lih, Lars T. 1987. "Gorbachev and the Reform Movement." *Current History* 86, 522 (October).

Litvin, Valentin. 1987. "Reforming Economic Management." *Problems of Communism* 36, 4 (July–August).

Lovenduski, Joni, and Woodall, Jean. 1987. *Politics and Society in Eastern Europe.* London: Macmillan.

Lynch, A. 1987. *The Soviet Study of International Relations.* Cambridge: Cambridge University Press.

————. 1989. *Gorbachev's International Outlook: Intellectual Origins and Political Consequences.* Occasional Papers Series #9, Institute for East-West Security Studies, New York.

Lyne, R. 1987. "Making Waves: Mr. Gorbachev's Public Diplomacy, 1985–6." *International Affairs* [London] 63, 2 (Spring).

Mandelbaum, M., and Talbott, S. 1986–87. "Reykjavik and Beyond." *Foreign Affairs*, Winter.

Mann, Dawn. 1988. "Paradoxes of Soviet Reform: The Nineteenth Communist Party Conference." Washington, D.C.: Significant Issues Series, Center for Strategic and International Studies.

Marcum, J. A. 1988/89. "Africa: A Continent Adrift." *Foreign Affairs* 68, 1.

Mastny, Vojtech, ed. 1987. *Soviet/East European Survey 1985–1986: Selected Research and Analysis from Radio Free Europe/Radio Liberty.* Durham, N.C.: Duke University Press.

————. 1988. "Europe in US-USSR Relations: A Topical Legacy." *Problems of Communism* 36, 1 (January–February).

Maynes, Charles William. 1987. "America's Chance." *Foreign Policy,* Fall.

MccGwire, M. 1987. "Update: Soviet Military Objectives." *World Policy Journal* 4, 4 (Fall).

McGovern, George. 1987/88. "The 1988 Election: U.S. Foreign Policy at a Watershed." *Foreign Affairs* 66, 3.

McNeill, T. 1987. "The USSR and Communism: The Twilight Years." *Radio Liberty Research Bulletin,* RL 428/87.

Meissner, Boris. 1985. "Soviet Policy: From Chernenko to Gorbachev." *Aussenpolitik* 36, 3.

————. 1986. "Gorbachev's Foreign Policy Programme." *Aussenpolitik* 37, 2.

————. 1987. "Gorbachev's Perestroika: Reform or Revolution?" *Aussenpolitik* 38.

Mertes, Alois. 1985. "Nuclear War in the Military Doctrine of the USSR." *Aussenpolitik* 36.

Miller, J. F. 1988. "The Geographical Disposition of the Soviet Armed Forces." *Soviet Studies* 40, 3 (July).

Miller, R. F. 1988. "Gorbachev's 'New Thinking': The Diplomatic and Military Implications." *Quadrant* 32, 7, no. 296 (July).

"Moscow's Foreign Policy Initiatives." 1986. *Soviet Analyst* 15, 16 (13 August).

Nahaylo, Bohdan. 1986a. "The Soviet Military and the Kremlin's Moratorium on Nuclear Tests." *Radio Liberty Research Bulletin,* RL 381/86.

————. 1986b. "Soviet Foreign Policy during Gorbachev's First Year." *Radio Liberty Research Bulletin,* RL 78/86.

————. 1986c. "Gorbachev Takes a Closer Look at Asia and the Pacific from Vladivostok." *Radio Liberty Research Bulletin,* RL 294/86.

————. 1986d. "New Pragmatism in Soviet Foreign Policy?" *Radio Liberty Research Bulletin,* RL 369/86.

————. 1986e. "Gorbachev's Speech to the Twenty-Seventh Party Congress: Superficial Treatment of Foreign Policy Issues." *Radio Liberty Research Bulletin,* RL 98/86.

————. 1987. "Towards a Settlement of the Afghanistan Conflict: A Chronological Overview." *Radio Liberty Research Bulletin,* 16/87.

Nations, R. 1986. "Moscow's New Tack." *Far Eastern Economic Review* 133 (August).

Neidl, R., and Boserup, A. 1987. "Beyond INF: A New Approach to Non-nuclear Forces." *World Policy Journal* 4, 4 (Fall).

Nichols, T. M. 1987. "The Military and 'The New Political Thinking': Lizichev on Leninism and Defence." *Radio Liberty Research Bulletin*, 26 February.

Nicholson, M. 1986. "Gorbachev's First Congress." *The World Today*, February.

Nixon, R. 1988/89. "American Foreign Policy: The Bush Agenda." *Foreign Affairs* 68, 1.

Nove, Alec. 1987. "Radical Reform: Problems and Prospects." *Soviet Studies* 39, 3 (July).

Odom, W. E. 1987. "How Far Can Soviet Reform Go?" *Problems of Communism* 36, 6 (November–December).

————. 1989. "Soviet Military Doctrine." *Foreign Affairs* 68.

Petersen, P. A., and Trulock, N. 1988. "A 'New' Soviet Military Doctrine: Origins and Implications." *Strategic Review*, Summer.

Pick, Otto. 1987. "How Serious Is Gorbachev about Arms Control?" *The World Today*, April.

Pipes, Richard. 1988. What Divides Us?" *Moscow News*, 22 May.

Quigley, J. 1988. "*Perestroika* and International Law." *American Journal of International Law* 82, 4 (October).

Rahr, Alexander. 1986. "Winds of Change Hit Foreign Ministry." *Radio Liberty Research Bulletin*, RL 274/86, 16 July.

Reddaway, P. 1988. "Resisting Gorbachev." *New York Review of Books*, 18 August.

Regnard, Henri. 1987. "Soviet Gains from Intelligence Gathering in the West." *Aussenpolitik* 38.

Roeder, P. G. 1985. "Do New Soviet Leaders Really Make a Difference? Rethinking the 'Succession Connection.'" *American Political Science Review* 79, 4 (December).

Rubinstein, Alvin Z. 1986. "A Third World Policy Waits for Gorbachev." *Orbis* 30, 2 (Summer).

————. 1988. "Soviet Success Story: The Third World." *Orbis* 32, 4 (Fall).

Rumer, Boris. 1986. "Realities of Gorbachev's Economic Program." *Problems of Communism* 35, 3 (May–June).

Scanlan, James P. 1988. "Reforms and Civil Society in the USSR." *Problems of Communism* 37, 2 (March–April).

Schemann, S.; Markham, J. M.; and Kaufman, M. T. 1989. "Communism Now: What Is It?" *New York Times*, January 22, 23, 24.

Sestanovich, Stephen. 1988a. "Gorbachev's Foreign Policy: A Diplomacy of Decline." *Problems of Communism* 37, 1 (January–February).

————. 1988b. "Gorbachev: Giving Away The Store?" *Washington Post*, 11 December.

Sharansky, Natan. 1988. "As I See Gorbachev." *Commentary*, March.

Shelton, Judy. 1989. *The Coming Soviet Crash: Gorbachev's Desperate Pursuit of Credit in Western Financial Markets*. New York: Free Press.

Shenfield, Stephen. 1987. *The Nuclear Predicament: Explorations in Soviet Ideology*. Chatham House Paper 37. London: Routledge and Kegan Paul.

Shlapentokh, Vladimir. 1985. "Two Levels of Public Opinion: The Soviet Case." *Public Opinion Quarterly*, Winter.

―――. 1988. "The XXVII Congress—A Case Study of the Shaping of a New Party Ideology." *Soviet Studies* 40, 1 (January).

Shulman, Marshall D., ed. 1986. *East-West Tensions in the Third World*. New York: W. W. Norton.

Shulman, M. D. 1987/88. "The Superpowers: Dance of the Dinosaurs." *Foreign Affairs* 66, 3.

Simes, Dimitri K. 1987. "Gorbachev: A New Foreign Policy?" *Foreign Affairs* 65, 3.

Simis, K. 1985. "The Gorbachev Generation." *Foreign Policy*, Summer.

Snyder, Jack. 1987/88. "The Gorbachev Revolution: A Waning of Soviet Expansionism?" *International Security* 12, 3 (Winter).

―――. 1988. "Limiting Offensive Conventional Forces: Soviet Proposals and Western Options." *International Security* 12, 4 (Spring).

Soviet Union in the 1980s. 1984. Proceedings of the Academy of Political Science.

Staar, Richard F. 1987. *USSR Foreign Policies After Detente*. Stanford: Hoover Institution Press.

Starr, S. Frederich. 1988. "Soviet Union: A Civil Society." *Foreign Policy* 70 (Spring).

Stern, G. 1984. "Soviet Foreign Policy in the 1980s." *Millennium* 13, 3.

Stewart, P. D. 1986. "Gorbachev and Obstacles Toward Detente." *Political Science Quarterly* 101, 1.

Svec, Milan. 1987–88. "Removing Gorbachev's Edge." *Foreign Policy* 69 (Winter).

Tatu, Michel. 1987. "Seventy Years after the Revolution: What Next?" *Radio Liberty Research Bulletin*, RL 426.

Tedstrom, John E. 1987. "Analyzing the 'Basic Provisions.'" *Problems of Communism* 36, 4 (July–August).

Teague, E. 1986a. "Gorbachev and Ligachev on 'The Struggle of Ideas' in the USSR." *Radio Liberty Research Bulletin*, RL 379/86 (October).

―――. 1986b. "Gorbachev's Ideological Platform Takes Shape." *Radio Liberty Research Bulletin*, RL 368/86 (September).

Tismaneanu, Vladimir. 1986a. "Neo-Stalinism and Reform Communism." *Orbis* 30, 2 (Summer).

————. 1986b. "Limits of Critical Marxism." *Problems of Communism* 35, 1 (January–February).

————. 1987. "Pitfalls of Detente." *Problems of Communism* 36, 3 (May–June).

Tolz, V. 1987. "Gorbachev Lays Down Official Line on Stalin's Legacy." *Radio Liberty Research Bulletin*, RL 431/87 (November).

Tucker, R. C. 1987a. *Political Culture and Leadership in Soviet Russia: From Lenin to Gorbachev.* London: Wheatsheaf Books.

————. 1987b. "Gorbachev and the Fight for Soviet Reform." *World Policy Journal* 4, 2 (Spring).

————. 1988/89. "Reagan's Foreign Policy." *Foreign Affairs* 68, 1.

Urban, George. 1988. "Should We Help Gorbachev?" *The World Today* 44, 2 (February).

Valkenier, E. K. 1986. "Revolutionary Change in the Third World." *World Politics* 38, 3 (April).

————. 1987. "New Soviet Thinking about the Third World." *World Policy Journal* 4, 4.

Volgyes, Ivan. 1986. "Troubled Friendship or Mutual Dependence? Eastern Europe and the USSR in the Gorbachev Era." *Orbis* 30, 2 (Summer).

Walker, M. 1987. "Gorbachev Speech a Major Change in Soviet Ideology." *The Guardian Weekly*, 1 March.

Weinberger, C. W. 1988. "Arms Reductions and Deterrence." *Foreign Affairs* 66, 4 (Spring).

Wettig, Gerhard. 1985. "The Soviet Union and Arms Control." *Aussenpolitik* 36.

————. 1986. *Sicherheit über alles—Krieg und Frieden in Sowjetischer Sicht.* Cologne: Markus Verlag.

————. 1987a. "Gorbachev and 'New Thinking' in the Kremlin's Foreign Policy." *Aussenpoliitk* 38, 2.

————. 1987b. "Gorbachev's Strategies for Disarmament and Security." *Aussenpolitik* 38 (January).

————. 1987c. "Has Soviet Military Doctrine Changed?" *Radio Liberty Research Bulletin*, 20 November.

————. 1988a. "Europe After the INF Treaty." *Aussenpolitik* 39, 1.

————. 1988b. "'New Thinking' on Security." *Problems of Communism* 37 (March–April).

————. 1988c. "New Development of Soviet Military Doctrine." *Aussenpolitik* 39, 2.

Witte, Barthold C. 1988. "A New Start for the UNESCO." *Aussenpolitik* 39, 1.

Wolfe, Alan. 1979. *The Rise and Fall of the 'Soviet Threat': Domestic Sources of the Cold War Consensus.* Washington, D.C.: Institute for Political Studies.

Wolfson, Z. 1987. "Some Environmental and Social Aspects of Nuclear Power Development in the USSR." Hebrew University of Jerusalem, Research Paper No. 63, March.

Yasman, V. 1987. "Ideologists Attempt to Explain Restructuring and Acceleration." *Radio Liberty Research Bulletin*, RL 179/87.

Young, P. 1987. "Gorbachev's Pacific Ambitions: The Soviets Are Here to Stay." *Pacific Islands Monthly.*

Zagoria, D. S. 1988/89. "Soviet Policy in East Asia: A New Beginning?" *Foreign Affairs* 68, 1.

Zhi, Rong, and Zhang, Wuzhuan. 1988. "Gorbachev's 'New Thinking' and Foreign Policy Adjustments." *Beijing Review*, 15–21 August.

Zinoviev, Alexander. 1986. *Die Macht des Unglaubens: Anmerkungen zur Soviet-Ideologie.* Munich/Zurich: Piper.

Appendix 3

NEW THINKING'S WHO'S WHO:
Major Figures Involved in the Conception and Implementation of New Thinking

Adamishin, A.	Deputy Foreign Minister
Adamovich, A.	Professor and corresponding member, Byelorussian Academy of Sciences
Afanaseyev, V. G.	Editor, *Pravda*; member, Ideological Commission of the CPSU; member, CPSU Central Committee
Akhromeyev, S. F.	Aide to Gorbachev; formerly Chief of General Staff [replaced by M. Moiseyev]
Arbatov, A. G.	Head of department, Institute of World Economy and International Relations (IMEMO)
Arbatov, Academician G. A.	Director, Institute of USA and Canada, USSR Academy of Sciences; member, Commission on Issues of International Policies; member, CPSU Central Committee; member, UN "Palme Commission"
Bovin, A.	Political commentator, *Izvestiya*
Brutens, K.	First Deputy Chief, International Department, CPSU Central Committee
Burlatsky, F. M.	Political commentator, *Literaturnaia gazeta*; head, Department of Philosophy, Central Committee Institute of Social Sciences; Vice President, Soviet Political Science Association
Bykov, O. N.	Deputy Director, Institute of World Economy and International Relations
Chernyayev, A.	Gorbachev's foreign policy aide
Dobrynin, A. F.	Chairman, Foreign Affairs Commission, USSR Supreme Soviet Council of Nationalities; formerly Secretary, CPSU Central Committee;

	formerly head, International Department, CPSU Central Committee; formerly Ambassador to the USA
Falin, V.	Head, International Relations Department, CPSU Central Committee [under Yakovlev]; member, Central Committee; formerly chief, Novosti Agency; formerly Ambassador to Bonn
Fedoseyev, Academician P. N.	Vice-President, USSR Academy of Sciences; formerly director, Institute of Philosophy and of Central Committee Institute of Marxism-Leninism
Frolov, Academician I. T.	Member, CPSU Central Committee; aide to General Secretary, CPSU Central Committee; formerly chief editor, *Kommunist*; Vice-President, USSR Academy of Sciences; chairman, Scientific Council, Academy of Sciences on Philosophical and Social Problems of Science and Technology; formerly chief editor, *Voprosy filosofii*
Gareyev, M. A.	Deputy Chief of General Staff; leading military theoretician
Gerasimov, G.	Chief, USSR Foreign Ministry Information Administration
Gorbachev, M. S.	General Secretary, CPSU Central Committee; chairman of the Presidium of the Supreme Soviet of the USSR (President of the USSR)
Gromyko, Anatolii	[Son of Andrei] Director, Africa Institute, USSR Academy of Sciences
Gromyko, Andrei	[Father of Anatolii] Formerly Foreign Minister; formerly President of the USSR
Ivanov, I. D.	Head, International Economics Department, Ministry of Foreign Affairs; formerly deputy director, Institute of World Economy and International Relations
Kapto, A.	Member, CPSU Central Committee; head, Central Committee ideological department
Karpov, V.	Deputy Foreign Minister
Kortunov, A. V.	Institute of USA and Canada Studies, USSR Academy of Sciences

Krasin, Y.	Pro-Rector of the Central Committee Academy of Social Sciences
Kryuchkov, V.	Chairman, KGB
Ligachev, Y. K.	Member of Politburo in charge of agriculture; Secretary, CPSU Central Committee; formerly chairman, Ideological Commission
Lizichev, A. D.	Army general; Chief, Main Political Directorate of the Soviet Army and Navy; member, CPSU Central Committee
Lomeiko, V.	Journalist; ambassador at large; permanent representative at UNESCO
Lushev, P.	Military commander of the Warsaw Pact; formerly USSR Deputy Minister of Defense
Medevedev, V. A.	Chairman, Ideological Commission, CPSU Central Committee; member of Politburo
Melville, A. Y.	Section head, Institute of USA and Canada Studies, USSR Academy of Sciences
Plimak, Y.	Historian and theorist at Institute of International Workers' Movement; formerly at Institute of Philosophy
Petrovsky, V.	Deputy Foreign Minister
Primakov, Academician E. M.	Secretary of branch of USSR Academy of Sciences for "Problems of World Economy and International Relations," established to coordinate seven research institutes (World Economy and International Relations, USA and Canada, International Workers' Movement, Europe, Eastern Studies, Africa, Latin America); director, Institute of World Economy and International Relations (IMEMO); formerly director, Institute of Oriental Studies; member, CPSU Central Committee
Rusakov, K. V.	Formerly Secretary of CPSU Central Committee; formerly head, Department for Liaison with Communist and Workers' Parties of Socialist Countries, CPSU Central Committee
Ryzhkov, N. V.	USSR Chairman of Council of Ministers; member of Politburo

Shakhnazarov, G. K.	Aide to Gorbachev; chairman, Soviet Political Science Association; formerly first deputy head, Central Committee Department for Liaison with Communist and Workers' Parties of Socialist Countries (now absorbed in International Department); professor of political science
Shevardnadze, E. A.	Minister of Foreign Affairs; member of Politburo
Smirnov, G. L.	Director, Institute of Marxism-Leninism of CPSU Central Committee; candidate member, CPSU Central Committee; member, Ideological Commission of Central Committee; formerly director, Institute of Philosophy, USSR Academy of Sciences
Sokolov, Marshal S. L.	Formerly Minister of Defense
Timofeyev, T. T.	Historian and economist; director, Institute of International Workers' Movement
Trofimenko, G. A.	Head, Department of US Foreign Policy, Institute of International Workers' Movement
Yakovlev, A. N.	Member of Politburo; chairman, Commission of CPSU Central Committee on Issues of International Policies; Secretary of the Central Committee; formerly head, Propaganda Department of the Central Committee; formerly deputy head, Department of Science and Culture of the Central Committee (1965–73); formerly Ambassador to Canada (1973–83); formerly director, Institute of World Economy and International Relations (IMEMO) (1983–85)
Yakovlev, E.	Editor, *Moscow News* (after Gennadi Gerasimov)
Yazov, D. T.	Minister of defense; member of Politburo
Zagladin, Vadim V.	Aide to Gorbachev; secretary, Foreign Affairs Committee of the USSR Supreme Soviet Council of the Union; formerly first deputy head, International Department, CPSU Central Committee (with special responsibility for Western Europe)
Zhilin, Y. A.	Head, group of consultants on foreign policy to CPSU Central Committee

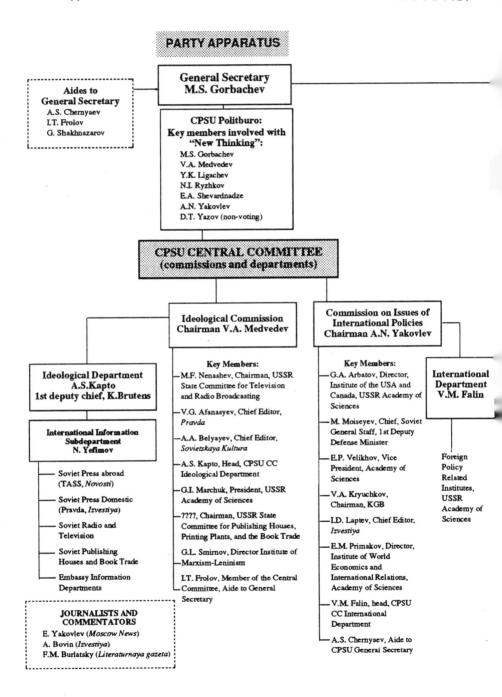

PARTY APPARATUS

Aides to General Secretary
A.S. Chernyaev
I.T. Frolov
G. Shakhnazarov

General Secretary M.S. Gorbachev

CPSU Politburo:
Key members involved with "New Thinking":
M.S. Gorbachev
V.A. Medvedev
Y.K. Ligachev
N.I. Ryzhkov
E.A. Shevardnadze
A.N. Yakovlev
D.T. Yazov (non-voting)

CPSU CENTRAL COMMITTEE (commissions and departments)

Ideological Commission Chairman V.A. Medvedev

Commission on Issues of International Policies Chairman A.N. Yakovlev

Ideological Department A.S.Kapto 1st deputy chief, K.Brutens

International Information Subdepartment N. Yefimov

— Soviet Press abroad (TASS, *Novosti*)

— Soviet Press Domestic (Pravda, *Izvestiya*)

— Soviet Radio and Television

— Soviet Publishing Houses and Book Trade

— Embassy Information Departments

Key Members:
— M.F. Nenashev, Chairman, USSR State Committee for Television and Radio Broadcasting

— V.G. Afanasyev, Chief Editor, *Pravda*

— A.A. Belyayev, Chief Editor, *Sovietskaya Kultura*

— A.S. Kapto, Head, CPSU CC Ideological Department

— G.I. Marchuk, President, USSR Academy of Sciences

— ????, Chairman, USSR State Committee for Publishing Houses, Printing Plants, and the Book Trade

— G.L. Smirnov, Director Institute of Marxism-Leninism

— I.T. Frolov, Member of the Central Committee, Aide to General Secretary

Key Members:
— G.A. Arbatov, Director, Institute of the USA and Canada, USSR Academy of Sciences

— M. Moiseyev, Chief, Soviet General Staff, 1st Deputy Defense Minister

— E.P. Velikhov, Vice President, Academy of Sciences

— V.A. Kryuchkov, Chairman, KGB

— I.D. Laptev, Chief Editor, *Izvestiya*

— E.M. Primakov, Director, Institute of World Economics and International Relations, Academy of Sciences

— V.M. Falin, head, CPSU CC International Department

— A.S. Chernyaev, Aide to CPSU General Secretary

International Department V.M. Falin

Foreign Policy Related Institutes, USSR Academy of Sciences

JOURNALISTS AND COMMENTATORS
E. Yakovlev (*Moscow News*)
A. Bovin (*Izvestiya*)
F.M. Burlatsky (*Literaturnaya gazeta*)

FOREIGN POLICY AND IDEOLOGY ESTABLISHMENTS

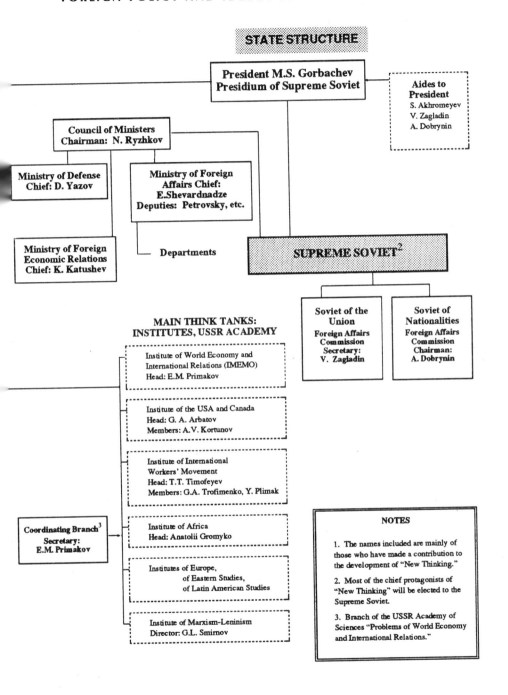

STATE STRUCTURE

President M.S. Gorbachev
Presidium of Supreme Soviet

Aides to President
S. Akhromeyev
V. Zagladin
A. Dobrynin

Council of Ministers
Chairman: N. Ryzhkov

Ministry of Defense
Chief: D. Yazov

Ministry of Foreign
Affairs Chief:
E.Shevardnadze
Deputies: Petrovsky, etc.

Ministry of Foreign
Economic Relations
Chief: K. Katushev

Departments

SUPREME SOVIET[2]

Soviet of the Union
Foreign Affairs Commission
Secretary:
V. Zagladin

Soviet of Nationalities
Foreign Affairs Commission
Chairman:
A. Dobrynin

**MAIN THINK TANKS:
INSTITUTES, USSR ACADEMY**

Institute of World Economy and
International Relations (IMEMO)
Head: E.M. Primakov

Institute of the USA and Canada
Head: G. A. Arbatov
Members: A.V. Kortunov

Institute of International
Workers' Movement
Head: T.T. Timofeyev
Members: G.A. Trofimenko, Y. Plimak

Institute of Africa
Head: Anatolii Gromyko

Coordinating Branch[3]
Secretary:
E.M. Primakov

Institutes of Europe,
of Eastern Studies,
of Latin American Studies

Institute of Marxism-Leninism
Director: G.L. Smirnov

NOTES

1. The names included are mainly of those who have made a contribution to the development of "New Thinking."

2. Most of the chief protagonists of "New Thinking" will be elected to the Supreme Soviet.

3. Branch of the USSR Academy of Sciences "Problems of World Economy and International Relations."

Pravda [25 August 1987]: The favorite stamp of the Pentagon classifying Soviet peace initiatives as "Soviet Propaganda."

Pravda [5 May 1987]: Cyclists on "Progressive Western Press" machines smile at their colleague getting nowhere on his stationary "anti-Sovietism" rig: "Time you got yourself a bicycle, mate."

Pravda [27 August 1987]: A crane-truck with the inscription "New Thinking" lifts the planet from quicksand of weapons.

Pravda [19 October 1987]: The sun of "Openness/New Thinking/Restructuring" shines on the melting snowman "Cold War."

Pravda [16 December 1987]: A smiling globe, with a palette labelled "New Thinking," paints a sunny pastoral scene to replace bombs and missiles.

Pravda [17 December 1987]: Voice from the wagon of the "Soviet Threat Circus," deserted by horse and audience perusing "Perestroika in the USSR" and "New Thinking": "It seems we can't go much further."

Pravda [16 February 1988]: "Scrapheap"—The magnet of "New Thinking" removes the armor of Mars and disarms him.

Pravda [21 February 1988]: "Reliable Remedies"—"What have you been up to?" asks Dr. New Thinking of the injured planet. The medical history reads "1. Arms race; 2. Regional conflict; 3. Famine; 4. Poverty; 5. Illiteracy; 6. Ecological problems." Saying "These medications will put you on your feet fast," the doctor prescribes "Consultations, Disarmament, Trust."

Pravda [6 March 1988]: "Masters of 'Original' Thinking."—Alarmed by radio and TV reports of "Perestroika in the USSR" and "Glasnost in the USSR," a Reagan look-alike is obliged to read about "New Political Thinking." His response is to draw a bomb labelled "Glasnost/Perestroika/New Thinking" and then comment: "As you can see, we face a new Soviet threat!!"

Pravda [24 May 1988]: A smiling planet mounted on "New Thinking" clears the obstacles of "mutual mistrust," "image of the enemy," "hostility," and "suspicion."

Pravda [27 May 1988]: "If Only the World Could Cooperate"—The planet climbs up the stepladder from Geneva to Reykjavik to Washington to Moscow to repair the structural flaws caused by "mistrust," "conflict," "confrontation," and "threat."

VENDULKA KUBÁLKOVÁ, originally from Czechoslovakia, has doctorates from both the East (D.Jur., Charles University, Prague) and from the West (Ph.D., Lancaster, England). After fifteen years in Australia (Australian National University and the University of Queensland), she is now Professor of International Studies at the Graduate School of International Studies, University of Miami, Florida.

ALBERT ANDERSON CRUICKSHANK was educated at Glasgow (M.A.) and Oxford (D.Phil.) and has taught international relations in American, Turkish, and New Zealand universities.

Works co-authored by Kubálková and Cruickshank include *Marxism-Leninism and Theory of International Relations* (Routledge and Kegan Paul, London and Boston, 1980), *International Inequality* (Croom Helm and St. Martin's Press, London and New York, 1981), and *Marxism and International Relations* (Clarendon Press, Oxford and New York, 1985; published in revised form in 1989 as an Oxford Paperback).

INSTITUTE OF INTERNATIONAL STUDIES
UNIVERSITY OF CALIFORNIA, BERKELEY

215 Moses Hall   Berkeley, California 94720

CARL G. ROSBERG, Director

Monographs published by the Institute include:

RESEARCH SERIES

16. *The International Imperatives of Technology.* Eugene B. Skolnikoff. ($2.95)
21. *The Desert & The Sown: Nomads in Wider Society.* Ed. C. Nelson. ($5.50)
22. *U.S.-Japanese Competition in International Markets.* J. E. Roemer. ($3.95)
24. *Urban Inequality and Housing Policy in Tanzania.* Richard E. Stren. ($2.95)
25. *The Obsolescence of Regional Integration Theory.* Ernst B. Haas. ($6.95)
27. *The SOCSIM Microsimulation Program.* E. A. Hammel et al. ($4.50)
28. *Authoritarian Politics in Communist Europe.* Ed. Andrew C. Janos. ($8.95)
32. *Agricultural Policy and Performance in Zambia.* Doris J. Dodge. ($4.95)
34. *Housing the Urban Poor in Africa.* Richard E. Stren. ($5.95)
35. *The Russian New Right: Right-Wing Ideologies in the USSR.* A. Yanov. ($5.95)
37. *The Leninist Response to National Dependency.* Kenneth Jowitt. ($4.95)
38. *Socialism in Sub-Saharan Africa.* Eds. C. Rosberg & T. Callaghy. ($12.95)
39. *Tanzania's Ujamaa Villages: Rural Development Strategy.* D. McHenry. ($5.95)
43. *The Apartheid Regime.* Eds. R. Price & C. Rosberg. ($12.50)
44. *Yugoslav Economic System in the 1970s.* Laura D. Tyson. ($5.95)
46. *Conflict and Coexistence in Belgium.* Ed. Arend Lijphart. ($10.50)
47. *Changing Realities in Southern Africa.* Ed. Michael Clough. ($12.50)
48. *Nigerian Women Mobilized, 1900–1964.* Nina E. Mba. ($12.95)
49. *Institutions of Rural Development.* Eds. D. Leonard & D. Marshall. ($11.50)
50. *Politics of Women & Work in the USSR & the U.S.* Joel C. Moses. ($9.50)
51. *Zionism and Territory.* Baruch Kimmerling. ($13.95)
52. *Soviet Subsidization of Trade with East Europe.* M. Marrese/J. Vanous. ($14.50)
53. *Voluntary Efforts in Decentralized Management.* L. Ralston et al. ($10.00)
54. *Corporate State Ideologies.* Carl Landauer. ($5.95)
55. *Effects of Economic Reform in Yugoslavia.* John P. Burkett. ($9.50)
56. *The Drama of the Soviet 1960s.* Alexander Yanov. ($9.50)
57. *Revolutions & Rebellions in Afghanistan.* Eds. Shahrani/Canfield. ($14.95)
58. *Women Farmers of Malawi.* D. Hirschmann & M. Vaughan. ($8.95)
59. *Chilean Agriculture under Military Rule.* Lovell S. Jarvis. ($11.50)
60. *Influencing Political Behavior in the Netherlands and Austria.* J. Houska. ($11.50)
61. *Social Policies in Western Industrial Societies.* C. F. Andrain. ($14.50)
62. *Comparative Social Policy.* Harold Wilensky et al. ($7.50)
63. *State-Building Failure in Ireland and Algeria.* I. Lustick. ($8.95)
64. *Social Legislation in Middle East.* Eds. Michalak/Salacuse. ($15.50)
65. *Foreign Politics of Richard Nixon.* Franz Schurmann. ($18.50)
66. *State, Oil, & Agriculture in Nigeria.* Ed. Michael Watts. ($16.95)
67. *Apartheid in a South African Town.* Martin West. ($9.50)
68. *International Politics of Telecommunications.* D. Blatherwick. ($8.95)

LIST OF PUBLICATIONS (*continued*)

69. *Democratic Corporatism & Policy Linkages.* H. Wilensky/L. Turner. ($8.00)
70. *Technology, Competition & the Soviet Bloc.* K. Poznanski. ($13.95)
71. *State & Welfare, USA/USSR.* Eds. G. Lapidus & G. Swanson. ($22.50)
72. *Politics of Debt in Argentina, Brazil & Mexico.* R. Kaufman. ($9.50)
73. *No Longer an American Lake?* Ed. J. Ravenhill. ($14.95)

POLICY PAPERS IN INTERNATIONAL AFFAIRS

1. *Images of Detente & the Soviet Political Order.* K. Jowitt. ($1.250)
2. *Detente after Brezhnev: Domestic Roots of Soviet Policy.* A. Yanov. ($4.95)
3. *Mature Neighbor Policy: A New Policy for Latin America.* A. Fishlow. ($3.95)
4. *Five Images of Soviet Future: Review & Synthesis.* G. W. Breslauer. ($5.50)
5. *Global Evangelism: How to Protect Human Rights.* E. B. Haas. ($2.95)
6. *Israel & Jordan: An Adversarial Partnership.* Ian Lustick. ($2.00)
8. *U.S. Foreign Policy in Sub-Saharan Africa.* Robert M. Price. ($4.50)
9. *East-West Technology Transfer in Perspective.* R. J. Carrick. ($5.50)
11. *Toward Africanized Policy for Southern Africa.* R. Libby. ($7.50)
12. *Taiwan Relations Act & Defense of ROC.* Edwin K. Snyder et al. ($7.50)
13. *Cuba's Policy in Africa, 1959–1980.* William M. LeoGrande. ($4.50)
14. *Norway, NATO, & the Forgotten Soviet Challenge.* K. Amundsen. ($3.95)
15. *Japanese Industrial Policy.* Ira Magaziner and Thomas Hout. ($7.50)
16. *Containment, Soviet Behavior & Grand Strategy.* Robert Osgood. ($5.50)
17. *U.S.-Japanese Competition—Semiconductor Industry.* M. Borrus et al. (8.50)
18. *Contemporary Islamic Movements in Perspective.* Ira Lapidus. ($6.50)
19. *Atlantic Alliance, Nuclear Weapons, & European Attitudes.* W. Thies. ($4.50)
20. *War and Peace: Views from Moscow and Beijing.* B. Garrett & B. Glaser. ($7.95)
21. *Emerging Japanese Economic Influence in Africa.* J. Moss & J. Ravenhill. ($8.95)
22. *Nuclear Waste Disposal under the Seabed.* Edward Miles et al. ($7.50)
23. *NATO: The Tides of Discontent.* Earl Ravenal. ($7.50)
24. *Power-Sharing in South Africa.* Arend Lijphart. ($10.00)
25. *Reassessing the Soviet Challenge in Africa.* Ed. M. Clough. ($8.00)
26. *Why We Still Need the United Nations.* Ernst Haas. ($8.50)
27. *Impact of U.S. Policy in El Salvador.* M. Diskin & K. Sharpe. ($6.50)
28. *American Military Strategy.* Samuel P. Huntington. ($4.95)
29. *International Debt Threat.* Vinod K. Aggarwal. ($5.95)
30. *Nuclear Competition in South Asia.* R. R. Subramanian. ($5.50)
31. *Newly Industrializing Asia in Transition.* T. Cheng/S. Haggard. ($8.50)
32. *Asymmetries in Japanese-American Trade.* S. D. Krasner. ($6.50)
33. *Science, Politics & International Ocean Management.* E. Miles. ($6.50)
34. *Italian Communists vs. the Soviet Union.* J. Levesque. ($5.95)
35. *Large-Scale Foreign Policy Change: Nixon Doctrine.* E. Ravenal. ($8.50)

Modernization & Bureaucratic-Authoritarianism: Studies in South American Politics
Guillermo O'Donnell. ($9.50) [POM Series No. 9]